AVID

READER

PRESS

THESE WALLS

The Battle for
Rikers Island and
the Future of
America's Jails

EVA FEDDERLY

AVID READER PRESS
New York   London   Toronto   Sydney   New Delhi

Avid Reader Press
An Imprint of Simon & Schuster, Inc.
1230 Avenue of the Americas
New York, NY 10020

First Avid Reader Press hardcover edition October 2023

AVID READER PRESS and colophon are
trademarks of Simon & Schuster, Inc.

For information about special discounts for bulk purchases,
please contact Simon & Schuster Special Sales at
1-866-506-1949 or business@simonandschuster.com.

The Simon & Schuster Speakers Bureau can bring authors to
your live event. For more information or to book an event contact
the Simon & Schuster Speakers Bureau at 1-866-248-3049
or visit our website at www.simonspeakers.com.

Interior design by Lewelin Polanco

Manufactured in the United States of America

1 3 5 7 9 10 8 6 4 2

Library of Congress Cataloging-in-Publication Data has been applied for.

ISBN 978-1-9821-9391-1
ISBN 978-1-9821-9393-5 (ebook)

For the kids

What was true was also bottomless to contemplate.

—NORMAN MAILER, introduction
to *In the Belly of the Beast*

Contents

Author's Note

These Walls is based on four years of reporting, thousands of hours of research, multiple visits to detention centers, and over one hundred interviews. My journey began heading coverage for *Architectural Digest* on New York City's decision to close Rikers Island and build new jails in the boroughs. The initiative seemed like a powerful opportunity to dismantle one of America's largest and most expensive jails and reimagine the landscape of criminal justice. I also was fascinated by how we could use architecture as a means of reform. This set in motion an all-consuming quest that became *These Walls*.

To examine the contemporary, it's important to have an understanding of the past. Correctional architecture—its genesis, its goals, its development—is a surprisingly underexplored discipline in American history. I visited jails, prisons, courthouses, and museums; I read historical documents, archival meeting notes, legal documents, news articles, trade conference programs, white papers, and philosophical and trade books on the development of penal systems in the West. I worked with scholars, historians, architects, professors, jail staff, professional organizations, and nonprofit groups to get their insights and for corroboration of my research. The culmination of this work is a history of the evolution of correctional architecture in the United States, ending with recommendations about how we can move forward.

A quick note about language: while common parlance is to use the term *inmate*, various people and organizations consider it a derogatory and dehumanizing way to describe someone. In August 2021, New York State law made it official that people locked up are to be referred to as incarcerated individuals (though this law, signed by former New York governor Andrew Cuomo, is proving slow to catch on). As such, I use *incarcerated person*. The term *inmate* will be used only when I'm directly quoting someone.

An important decision I made when writing *These Walls* was to present myriad perspectives from people who've experienced the justice system in some way. Truth comes in many forms. One by one, incarcerated people, architects, prison abolitionists, judges, bureaucrats, law enforcement officials, nonprofit volunteers and employees, representatives of religious groups, attorneys, psychologists, environmentalists, and members of the community shared their experiences and feelings with me. By listening to those affected, I discovered we need to be asking bigger questions: What are our values? How do we define our ethics? What does "justice" look like? What are fundamental human rights? How can we do better? Do human beings belong in cells at all?

What constitutes "justice" is a broad, difficult, complex, and emotional subject. This book does not answer all the questions, but it aims to cast new light on some. I also present you with questions that I hope you'll want to consider. To address these, we need to better know our history, and we also need to learn by listening to others. We must examine our current processes and question our measures of reform. Only by digging in can we engage and move forward in a fruitful and effective way. As a pioneer in the Modern Movement in architecture, Eileen Gray, said: "To create, one must first question everything."

This is my invitation for you to join me.

THESE WALLS

ONE

Rikers Island

Our 21-minute call was almost up, but by now we were used to it. Every time Moose buzzed, the line was tapped. At least the call was free.

A dystopian haze had settled over New York City. Stoplights flicked from red to green to yellow, but there was no hum of cars, no symphony of horns at rush hour. Birds flew overhead, yet few planes soared through the open sky. The restaurants and theaters of Times Square were dark, but giant screens and billboards glowed like a scene out of a sci-fi thriller. It was 2020 and the COVID-19 pandemic had gripped the globe. Life, as we knew it, stood still.

Inside New York City's jails, life was far more unsettling. As the pandemic crawled on, my phone number slipped from cinderblock cell to cell, traveling like wildfire through the city's web of detention centers; daily dispatches were reported from the Manhattan Detention Complex, the Brooklyn Detention Complex, and the Vernon C. Bain Center, a looming barge floating off the coast of the South Bronx. Together, these jail facilities housed 2,500 beds. None was more dysfunctional, more problematic than Rikers Island, which at its peak in the 1990s warehoused over 21,000 people. Resting in the murky-green East River, this island houses not one but ten jails, eight of which are still active. Situated between the boroughs of Queens and the Bronx, Rikers—like all the city's jails—is governed by the New York City Department of Correction. Each day, this government agency transports about one tenth of Rikers' population to courthouses residing in the boroughs. (The city annually spends $31 million on these trips alone.) Even though Rikers rests just 100 yards from LaGuardia Airport's runways, this 413-acre island is completely isolated. Because of this, it's also self-sustaining, with its own bus depot, fire station, chapel, K9 unit, bakery, multiple trailers, a garden surrounded by razor wire, and a 30,000-square-foot power plant.

When the pandemic hit, jail programs shut down, visitors were barred from entering, mail delivery slowed, and basic services, like the jails' barber shops, shuttered, leaving people's hair and nails long and jagged. Some told me soap was scarce; social distancing, nearly impossible. Concrete cells were filled with fecal matter and urine, and some had inoperable sinks. Gnats circled rotting food on worn floors. People said they weren't given masks or hand sanitizer; Virex disinfectant was rarely distributed—one person said just every two weeks. Another reported that the George R. Vierno Center—one of Rikers' men's jails—was "the epicenter of the disease." It was like sitting on death row without a sentence.

We were in the early stages of the pandemic, in May 2020, when Moose first called. Protests over the recent murders of Ahmaud Arbery and George Floyd were crescendoing across the nation. Civil unrest shook the country, as the pandemic raged on. Citizens demanded we defund the police. New York City mayor Bill de Blasio would soon declare a state of emergency and issue a citywide curfew for the "health and welfare" of New Yorkers.

"This is a call from"—a man stated his name—"an incarcerated individual at the New York City Department of Correction," the automated announcement said.

A polite baritone voice came through the line and introduced himself. I was surprised by his cheerful disposition, despite the grim circumstances.

"Judges call me 'Jack.' Friends call me 'Moose.'" *

"How do you spell it?" I asked, grabbing a pen. "M-O-U-S-E?"

The voice let out a bellow of laughter, a Moose signature with which I became well acquainted. "Not like the dessert!"

I cracked a smile.

"Moose. M-O-O-S-E." He guffawed again.

When the pandemic first hit, Moose had been locked up on Rikers, the latest in his long string of stints in New York City's jail system. Owing to the pandemic, New York City—and other jurisdictions around the country—released people with "non-violent" charges.† New York City's total jail population dropped from 5,458 to 3,824, its lowest number since the 1940s. Among the released was Moose. He'd been roaming the Free World,

---

* His full name will not be used, to protect his privacy.

† Over the course of three weeks.

strolling the streets of the Bronx—homebase when he's not in the joint—where he rediscovered the rhythm of freedom.

"It felt so good to be out in the sunshine," Moose recalled. "Every day I was out in the sun, with Purell on my trigger finger."

Moose wasn't long for the Free World. While on the move, he misplaced his parole officer's phone number. He also got shot. "One bullet landed in my arm near my elbow," he said. "But I got an image to uphold in my neighborhood, so I laughed and drank beer." Less than three weeks later, the cops pinched him on 176th Street. He landed back in jail, the bullet still lodged in his arm.

"Sorry about your arm," I said. "You get it bandaged?"

"They haven't taken me to see anyone yet. I'm still waiting for them to wrap it." He paused. "I'm hoping to get released soon. Maybe Monday."

"Oh, wow, that soon."

His tone shifted to serious. "I heard you're writing a book about Rikers. How can I help?"

———

Rikers Island has many names: "Torture Island," "The Gladiator School," and the "House of Dead Men." During hot spells, it's "The Oven," since many cells lack air-conditioning. This island is one of the largest and most expensive jail complexes in the United States. Each jail on Rikers is defined by its own architecture, warden, staff, and people locked inside. There is one trait that most incarcerated people here share: most are untried.

Like the rest of America's jails, Rikers holds people who have not been convicted of a crime; they have not been sentenced. Though Americans are supposed to be presumed innocent until found guilty, jails are designed to hold those who have not yet seen their day in court. They wait, month after month, sometimes year after year, for their alleged constitutional right to a speedy trial. While prisons house those who've been convicted and sentenced with long-term, even lifetime stays (the longest sentence ever received was 10,000 years, according to *Guinness World Records*), jails remain, overwhelmingly, the institutions for those who can't afford bail (a small percentage of the population is serving sentences under one year). The justice system forces them to serve as human collateral behind these walls.

Though this is a crucial difference between a prison and a jail, the distinction is often not understood by those outside the criminal justice system. Some of America's most epic films, greatest writers, most respectable newspapers, and most prudent editors use the terms *jail* and *prison* interchangeably. Even today, when conversations about justice reform are at one of their most potent points, many members of the media and the public don't recognize the difference between a jail and a prison. To be clear, jails and prisons are not fungible. Many get this wrong from the start, revealing a frightening lack in awareness of how America's justice system actually works.

Some argue the system is designed to be opaque. The public and the media need not know what happens on the inside. Prisons and jails can sidestep First Amendment rights, leaving those who enter at the discretion of those at the helm of these institutions. Incarcerated people are given little contact with the outside world, some just in the form of lawyer visits and 21-minute phone calls. For visitors allowed inside, it can be like traveling through a byzantine maze, especially in places like Rikers.

Physically connecting Rikers to the Free World is just one lone bridge, dubbed the "Bridge of Pain" by rapper Flavor Flav, who did time here. To reach this island dedicated to mass incarceration, visitors wait on the Queens side at the foot of the bridge, at a public bus stop. After picking up anyone there, the Q100 rumbles across the two-lane bridge. On Rikers, the bus empties its passengers, typically wives, girlfriends, children, extended family members, and friends. Correction officers in street clothes and program and nonprofit volunteers also ride. Although it's just a four-minute drive, Rikers feels like a different world.

Visitors wait in a seemingly endless line to pass through the first security checkpoint. After more waits and delays, they board a second bus—a white Department of Correction (DOC) vehicle with metal-grate-covered windows—which moves them to the specific jail they're visiting. Here, they undergo another round of security checks. Diapers, food, money, purses, and reading materials must be checked in lockers at a visitor waiting area. These visits are limited to certain hours, three times a week, and only on weekdays. The visitors then must wait for the Q100's return ride to Queens to go home to the Free World. Though visits are capped at one hour, a trip to Rikers can take all day. Like so many other jails and prisons, this world of detention is tucked away and out of reach. Obviously, Rikers was not designed to keep families intact.

For those in jail, three out of four are locked up because they don't have the cash to buy their freedom. Those who've got the scratch—like Harvey Weinstein, who posted a $1 million bail on his rape charges—pay the price and hang out in the Free World until their court date. If they have some cash, they can visit a bail-bond shop, which are posted up opportunistically around the nation's courthouses and jails. Bail bondsmen lend cash bail for sky-high, nonrefundable premiums. The average bail runs around $10,000, equal to about eight months' pay for the typical detainee. For most, the cost of freedom is prohibitive. Those with little means must serve as collateral themselves. They're locked in jail, where they languish, waiting for their scheduled time in a legal system that's a tangle of arcane hurdles and long delays. When their day in court does arrive—whether they're found guilty or not guilty—they've been stripped from their families, removed from their jobs or schools, and severed from their responsibilities. A survey found that, on one day in New York City in 2022, untried people were being held in jail for an average of 286 days while awaiting their court dates. (Those who received mental health services while in jail were likely to be held over for 50 percent longer time.) That's enough time for a person's life to fall apart.

This forced captivity mainly happens to people of color and those with little means. It is the default of America's criminal justice system. In New York City's jails, the vast number of incarcerated people are Black or Hispanic—to be specific, nine out of every ten. Nationally, Black people are incarcerated at a rate nearly six times that of white people; Hispanic people are three times as likely to be incarcerated as white people. Aside from the racial disparities in the justice system, incarceration is also extremely costly for taxpayers. In 2021, the city comptroller reported that to lock up one person for a year in a New York City jail, it costs over half a million dollars. To be exact: $556,539.

This extremely costly system is the nature of American justice. Jails account for far more people than America's prisons. Jails see over 10 million entries per year. The United States has about 3,116 local jails. That's a lot of people doing time, many of whom don't have convictions. Of all the people held in New York City jails, relatively few are sent to prison. Perhaps that's why there are significantly fewer prisons than jails. There are 1,566 state prisons—run by state governments—which incarcerate about 1 million people. Those who break federal laws are sent to one of the nation's 98 federal prisons. In 2022, federal prisons held 208,000 people.

A common belief is that private prisons are one of our justice system's biggest current problems. Though they certainly are problematic, private prisons locked up far fewer people than the nation's jails. Private prisons, run by for-profit corporations, accounted for only 8 percent of the nation's total incarcerated population in 2020. However, as of 2021, the Department of Justice is no longer allowed to contract out to privately operated prisons (though this rule does not apply to the many private facilities used by U.S. Immigration and Customs Enforcement, which falls under the management of the Department of Homeland

Security). As of the year 2023, there are 1,323 juvenile facilities, 181 immigration detention facilities, and 80 Indian country jails (there are also prisons in the U.S. territories, military prisons, state psychiatric hospitals, and civil commitment centers), according to the Prison Policy Initiative.

With so many people locked up in these institutions, America's incarceration rate is one of the highest in the world. We have more prisons and jails than we have colleges and universities. Despite the vast concentration of these facilities, many Americans remain untouched by the justice system. However—whether they know it or not—everybody has a jail nearby. With 3,116 local jails, that's roughly one per county. Jails are run by town sheriffs, wardens, or correction departments, each with its own set of rules, budgets, and philosophies. It's worth noting that even though incarceration is an integral part of our local, regional, and national infrastructure, there is no overarching body to monitor those jails, nor is there a nationwide database of local jail information. Only a periodic Census of Jails, prepared by the Bureau of Justice Statistics, can serve as a semi-consistent record. "I hate having to give this answer, but it's the truth: we don't know the answer, because there's no required reporting mechanism," a representative from the American Jail Association, a nonprofit organization for jail professionals, responded when I inquired about jail policies and national statistics. "Any numbers we have are just because people have chosen to give [them] to us."

Information we do have is on America's recidivism rate, meaning how frequently someone who's been released from detention is rearrested or locked up again. Our recidivism rate is one of the highest in the world: seven out of ten people[*] were rearrested within five years of release. Of all the arrests made in America, most (80 percent) are for low-level, nonviolent offenses. America's soaring incarceration and recidivism rates reveal that something isn't working.

To help make the nation safer, our communities stronger, and the incarcerated population closer to anything near international norms, we first must have a fundamental understanding of America's criminal justice system, its history, and how we got here. In the words of historian Arthur Schlesinger Jr., "History haunts even generations who refuse to learn history. Rhythms, patterns, continuities, drift out of time long forgotten to mold the present and to color the shape of things to come. . . . The dialectic between past and future will continue to form our lives. . . . The past helps explain where we are today and how we got there." Knowing our history can help prevent us from repeating the failures of our past, while informing our contemporary actions.

As one of America's largest, most dangerous jail complexes, Rikers Island embodies much of what's wrong with the current system. In 2022, its rampant violence and disorder brought Rikers to the brink of federal takeover. That year, 19 people on Rikers died while in custody. The majority of people locked up there are overwhelmingly Black and Brown, most of whom have not been convicted, unable to buy their way out. Through its architecture,

---

[*] Based on people released from state prisons; jails don't have overall reporting mechanisms.

its isolation, and its policies, Rikers has long personified the horrors of incarceration, but it hasn't always been this way.

=====

In 1664, when New Amsterdam became New York City, Rikers Island was owned by Dutch settler Abraham Rycken, who lived nearby in a home that survives today as the city's oldest inhabited house. At this time, Rikers was a small, marshy island, which was passed down, generation to generation, until 1884. That was the year the city paid $180,000 for the 87½ acres from Magistrate Richard Riker, a judge whose racist legacy includes sending free Black people back to the American South.

Around this same time, many of the city's incarcerated were held on another island, Blackwell's Island (today, Roosevelt Island), which housed a penitentiary, a hospital for "incurables," workhouses, and the reportedly filthy, abusive New York City Lunatic Asylum. The city was set on converting Rikers into a new place to hold some of the incarcerated population. First, Rikers would need to be expanded in size. Leveraging the labor of its imprisoned, the city expanded the island to 413 acres, using garbage and horse manure.

In 1933, the first jail opened on Rikers. Designed by Sloan & Robertson Architects, this Art Deco–style institution slept 1,200 people. The city's original goal was to transfer the Blackwell's population, slowly and partially, to Rikers. However, owing to a Blackwell's corruption scandal, that penitentiary was closed in 1935, causing all of the Blackwell's population to be hastily moved onto Rikers, the new hub for the city's castaways. The rancid smells emanating from the island were so pungent that when the 1939 World's Fair was to kick off in nearby Flushing, Queens, New Yorkers worried the odor would deter fair attendees. In an attempt to fight the fumes, the city planted a nursery on the island, but the baby trees' roots turned black and smelled acrid. When rats flooded the island to feast on the waste, the city unleashed dogs to try and wipe out the infestation. Today, rats still overrun the island.

The city was undeterred. New jails were opened across the island from the 1970s through the 1990s. All the jails were for men, except one—the Correctional Institution for Women, which opened in 1971. This women's jail was converted to a men's jail when the new women's jail opened in 1988, the Rose M. Singer Center. Painted a putrid shade of mauve pink, this jail came equipped with a 25-bed nursery for the babies of pregnant women (if the jail allows the mother to maintain custody, the baby can live here for up to a year).

Since the 1930s, multitudes of people have been locked in the jails of Rikers Island, including Tupac Shakur, Sid Vicious, Lil Wayne, Anna Sorokin, DMX, and Foxy Brown. New people enter, but the history remains. When the heat swells and the tide falls, the landfill's stench is a plaguing reminder that we haven't come far from the past.

In the 1970s and 1980s, Rikers came under fire when tough-on-crime policies locked away scores of people without convictions, leading to overpopulation, riots, and mistreatment. Twice, the city attempted to close Rikers, unsuccessfully: once in the late 1970s and again in the mid-2000s. As of 2023, Rikers is very much alive in the East River. Over the years, incarcerated people and correction officers have filed multiple lawsuits against the city. In 2015, the city settled a federal lawsuit concerning conditions at Rikers and acquiesced to numerous reforms. Rikers received a federal monitor, installed thousands of surveillance cameras, and restricted its staff from using force.

Though these reforms aimed to protect incarcerated people from violence, they did little to shield them from trauma. One 23-year-old painter told me about waiting for trial on Rikers in the fall of 2020, after an arrest for disorderly conduct. He couldn't afford bail and so was sent to Rikers, where he spent four months awaiting trial. While he was inside, he tested positive for COVID-19 and was quarantined with other sick men. (As of March 2023, in New York City jails, 15,158 staff and 11,991 incarcerated people got COVID-19; of them, 18 staff and 48 incarcerated people died.) The painter felt like he was losing his mind. He would try to immerse himself in a book, but setting it down would reignite the feeling of the walls closing in. Rikers, he and others believe, is haunted. When his court date arrived, the painter appeared before a judge and, like many others, he entered a guilty plea. Nearly all criminal cases (98 percent of federal criminal cases) are resolved with a plea bargain, a loophole used in criminal courts to speed up cases, whereby a defendant pleads guilty or no contest to obtain a lesser sentence. Ironically, almost no criminal defendants actually see their days in court. The painter was released. When we spoke two years later, he was still on parole. Recalling his time on Rikers, he burst into tears: "No one"—he wiped his cheeks— "should have to go through that."

There are countless stories like his, but there was one in particular that rose to national attention in 2015, again igniting calls for the closure of Rikers and prompting New York City's ban on solitary confinement of youths. In that year, after being held on Rikers for three years without a conviction, Kalief Browder, a 22-year-old Black man from the Bronx, killed himself.

As a high school sophomore, Browder was accused of stealing a backpack. The 16-year-old maintained his innocence. He'd had previous run-ins with the police: eight months before, he had taken a delivery truck for a joyride and crashed into another car, a crime for which he pled guilty and was put on probation, deemed a "youthful offender," meaning he wouldn't have a criminal record as a minor. For the backpack incident, the judge charged him with grand larceny, robbery, and assault, and his bail was set at $3,000. Browder's family eventually came up with the money through a bail bond, but Browder was denied release because he was on probation. Instead, the teenager was locked up on Rikers, due to a contemporaneous state law that offenders 16 years of age and older should be tried as adults. (New York was only one of two states to adhere to the practice, until it was ended with 2017's Raise the Age law.)

While at Rikers, Browder suffered multiple beatings from correction officers and other incarcerated people, and his trial was delayed over and over again. Prosecutors tried to convince him to take a plea deal for a two- to three-year sentence, but Browder understood that taking a plea deal would mean he'd forsake his right to a fair trial, and it would put a felony on his rap sheet. Browder spent more than 700 days in solitary confinement. He attempted suicide several times. Eventually, Browder's case was dismissed. He'd missed school for three years. After struggling with his mental health, two years after his release he hung himself at his mother's home.

The tragedy went public. Rikers surveillance footage of Browder's abuse was released. Nationwide, people saw inside Rikers. This young man's story was emblematic of what was wrong with America's criminal justice system: an untried child was removed from school to live at Rikers, waiting for his court date, for years. Rikers, once again, took the spotlight. People demanded change.

Among those advocating for change was New York City Council Speaker Melissa Mark-Viverito. In 2016, the speaker spotlighted Browder's tragedy in her State of the City address. Browder's mother, Venida, sat in the front row of the auditorium of a Bronx high school. Speaker Mark-Viverito told the packed audience that this loss of life embodied the failings of the criminal justice system, not just of New York City but also nationwide.

"Kalief entered as a child, but left as a broken man," Mark-Viverito said to the crowd. Browder's mom wiped tears from her eyes. "It is time to take our criminal justice system outside of the shadows and finally address the institutional racism which has plagued it for far too long." The auditorium erupted with applause. "It is time to reimagine our entire criminal justice system. . . . Rikers Island has come to represent our worst tendencies and our biggest failures. . . . For too long, Rikers has not stood for more justice, but for revenge. We must explore how we can get the population of Rikers to be so small that the dream of shutting it down becomes a reality."

Then came Mark-Viverito's headlining announcement.

She would launch an independent investigation of Rikers. Led by former chief judge of the State of New York Jonathan Lippman, the commission would have 27 members, including judges, lawyers, nonprofit leaders, and a real estate developer. The Independent Commission on New York City Criminal Justice and Incarceration Reform—nicknamed the "Lippman Commission"—would take the next year to develop a "community-based justice model that will complement existing reform efforts," Mark-Viverito declared. The launch of the Lippman Commission seemed well timed and attuned to the public's shifting perspectives of "justice."

Closing Rikers Island was political. Then New York governor Andrew Cuomo announced that his office was on board with the Lippman Commission's efforts. However, Bill de Blasio, the city's unpopular mayor, didn't seem to be. In early 2016, the mayor had told the press, "It would cost many billions of dollars, and I have to look out for what's feasible and I have to look out for the taxpayer." While the statement wasn't necessarily wrong, the mayor was growing out of step with many New Yorkers—and others around the country, who were rallying for change in the justice system. Across America, more philanthropic dollars were flowing into justice reform than ever before. Cities and towns were exploring creative answers to lower their jail populations, reform their sentencing policies, and improve the conduct of their police forces. The mood was ripe for change.

As the Lippman Commission began their interviews, studies, and research, Mayor de Blasio was facing pressure from numerous fronts. When the commission was gearing up to release its much-anticipated report, in an interesting turn of events, the mayor beat them to the punch. On Friday, March 31, 2017, de Blasio's team assembled a last-minute press conference at City Hall. The six-foot-five mayor stood in the grand marble rotunda, flanked by none other than Mark-Viverito and the director of the Mayor's Office of Criminal Justice, Elizabeth Glazer. The mayor's announcement that day would set the tone for criminal justice reform around the nation.

"New York City," de Blasio proclaimed to journalists, TV anchors, and cameras, "will close the Rikers Island jail facility." Cameras started clicking and flashing. "Rikers Island is an example and expression of a major national problem. The mass incarceration crisis did not begin in New York City, but it will end here. We are going to end the era of mass incarceration by making this important change."

While de Blasio didn't delve into details about how Rikers would close—aside from saying that it would slash its jail population through various reform measures—he did promise the closure of Rikers within ten years. Some were skeptical from the start, saying it was a publicity stunt from a feckless mayor attempting to score good PR, while others questioned how the mayor could possibly see the reform effort through, as he wouldn't be in office in ten years' time. How could he guarantee the next administration would accomplish this major initiative? Easy for him to announce the initiative, when it would be his successor's problem to solve. Still, others hoped this would be the greatest criminal justice overhaul the city had ever seen. Long-standing ethical questions could be addressed about jail conditions. People would no longer suffer on Rikers. New York City could be a pioneer in ending the nation's love affair with mass incarceration. This could be the beginning.

That same weekend, another press conference was held. The Lippman Commission released its first report, "A More Just New York City." After a year of research and listening to stakeholders and members of the community, the authors of the report proclaimed the Rikers closure as a "moral imperative." The commission suggested multiple reforms at various phases of the criminal justice process, such as bail reform, working with groups outside the jail system, and better training for correction officers. If the city could enact various reforms, the daily jail population at Rikers could drop to less than 5,000 over the next decade. (In 2017, the average daily population in the city's jails was 9,400 people.) Slowly, and one by one, the city could close each jail on Rikers, rendering the island empty within ten years. The newly available island could then be transformed into an extension of nearby LaGuardia Airport, or it could house next-generation or sustainable infrastructure. The city could also relocate some of its existing facilities in lower-income communities to Rikers Island, thereby freeing up space for parks, job training, and employment opportunities. A museum could be built on Rikers, dedicated to all who've suffered there.

The commission had another idea in store, one that would prove incendiary. Their idea positioned architecture at the forefront of justice reform. Rikers needs to close, yes, but new jails should be built in the boroughs. Brand-new, sleek detention centers designed by world-class architecture firms should replace the boroughs' older jails, such as the Tombs in Manhattan and The Boat in the East River. People inside could live in more "normalized" settings and be closer to the courthouses. These jails would be "humane," with natural sunlight, softer lighting, better acoustics, regular fixtures and furnishings, and temperature control that could reduce stress and encourage good behavior. The new façades could be welcoming and "inspire confidence in what happens inside," the Lippman Commission's report said. "Design has a direct impact on behavior," it proclaimed. "We know that jail design can actually help achieve better outcomes." These new jails would house fewer beds to keep the jail populations relatively small and to avoid overcrowding. Every jail could have a "town center" that offers social services. The environment, instead of punishing the incarcerated, could help them by supporting rehabilitation and thus reduce crime. New York City could become "a beacon of safety, humanity, and justice for cities across the country and around the world," the Lippman Report declared. "Let New York City lead the way, as it has done so often in the past." Fixing Rikers was impossible; these new jails could be the way of the future. They called it the Borough-Based Jails (BBJ) program.

"[Rikers] is the epitome of the mass incarceration model," Judge Jonathan Lippman told me. I thought about Moose and other people without sentences I talked to, sweating inside Rikers' old, fetid jails. "It puts a lot of people out of mind and out of sight and bad things happen. The people who work there are just as much in danger. You can't fix it or make it better. It's too entrenched in the mass incarceration mantra. You need a whole new approach, which is all about smaller, safer, and more humane jails." The new jails would provide a habitable space for incarcerated people, correction officers, and visitors. "Create the envelope to make the culture better. I think those go hand in hand. . . . You're not going to change Rikers in a fundamental way. Believe me, I've seen it all. Every time I go there, the city brings out a bunch of programs. The answer is to get rid of the godforsaken place. Get rid of that godforsaken place!"

In the early days of summer 2017, Mayor de Blasio formalized the Borough-Based Jails program. Some felt this could be de Blasio's mayoral legacy, a historic criminal justice overhaul that could inspire the nation. This wasn't the first time the city was attempting to be a national bellwether. New York City has paved the way for social change and progress; for instance, the first civil rights laws since Reconstruction were passed here, including those for fair housing, education, and employment, which inspired laws in dozens of others states. As E. B. White wrote in his book about New York City, *Here Is New York*, "It is to the nation what the white church spire is to the village, the visible symbol of aspiration and faith." While other cities around the nation were attempting their own sweeping criminal justice reform efforts, New York was in a unique situation— with fecund ground to experiment with justice reform. During the last 20 years, as many American cities experienced massive surges in their incarcerated populations, New York City saw the opposite: in just one generation, Gotham had transformed from an emblem of extreme urban disorder, earning its 1970s nickname "Fear City," into America's safest big city. Mayor de Blasio and the Lippman Commission were aiming for New York City to lead the way. The Borough-Based Jails program would have strong management, safe conditions, and a total of 3,544 jail beds and 380 secure hospital beds. Under "Smaller, Safer, Fairer: A Roadmap to Closing Rikers Island," Rikers Island would close entirely by 2026 (later pushed to August 31, 2027, ostensibly due to the pandemic and budget reasons, according to *Gothamist*).

To ensure successful execution, the city launched a Justice Implementation Task Force, chaired by Elizabeth Glazer and Zachary Carter, corporation counsel of the City of New York, to help shape the strategy for the new "smaller, safer and fairer" jail system. The new jails would be built in four of the city's five boroughs: Manhattan, Brooklyn, Queens, and the Bronx. (Staten Island would not be included, as the city determined it would not be cost-effective to build a jail there.)

This massive reform effort came at a hefty cost: $8.3 billion. The Lippman Commission and the City University of New York (CUNY)'s Institute for State and Local Governance said that it would ultimately save the city $2 billion a year in operating costs and would be paid for with 30-year bonds. Despite the high price tag, two years later the City Council voted in favor of the BBJ program. Rikers Island was mandated to close by 2027. The city was required by law to close each jail on Rikers and flip each jail over to the Department of Citywide Administrative Services. Legally, New York City would be prohibited from incarcerating people on Rikers Island after 2027. The overhaul was officially set in motion.

That's when I started covering the initiative for *Architectural Digest*. I wanted to explore whether this $8.3 billion was best spent on new jails, and whether architecture really could help solve America's mass-incarceration problem. Inherently, there is controversy surrounding reform, and soon I found that the Borough-Based Jails program was no different. Compelled to go beyond the scope of my assignments, I wanted perspectives from those on the ground—mainly, those who were incarcerated. Accustomed to working with attorneys from my staff days at *Courthouse News* (and growing up in my dad's law firm, where he practiced family law and criminal defense), I tracked down a group of young lawyers teaching debate to people on Rikers. Owing to the pandemic, Rikers Debate Project volunteers weren't allowed inside, and had thus pivoted to letter correspondence. The lawyer volunteers relayed my request to their students inside. That's when my phone started ringing daily—sometimes multiple times per day—with reports from behind the wall.

Moose caught word about a month in that there was a journalist looking to talk. He was back in the mix, except now he wasn't on Rikers. He was booked on a parole violation downtown at the Manhattan Detention Complex, colloquially called "the Tombs" because the original jail here emulated the ancient mausoleums of Egypt. The Tombs was one of the jails slated for demolition, to make way for a state-of-the-art, high-rise jail.

When Moose reached out to me, he was ready to talk. As a frequent flier, he knew the system well and wanted to share his thoughts on the inside. When I broached the subject of New

York City's plan to close Rikers Island and build new jails in the boroughs, his reaction shook me.

"Fuck, no! You can't get rid of the jails!" Moose hollered.

Before I could ask why not, the automated voice interrupted to tell us our time was up.

And the line clicked off.

TWO

Imprisonment

While *I awaited Moose's next call,* more incarcerated people used their minutes to share their feelings on closing Rikers, as well as their experiences inside. Some felt resigned, convinced that this is how the justice system would remain, that incarceration in America is inevitable.

However, it is not. Incarceration has not always been the main method of punishment. This style of discipline is a relatively new phenomenon, less than 200 years old. When colonizers' ships arrived on the coasts of the future United States, prisons weren't sitting there, waiting for them. They had to be conceptualized. They had to be designed and built.

At first, the colonizers had to follow their mother-country England's methods, mainly corporal and capital punishments. Yet after achieving independence, the young nation had a rare opportunity to fashion a new republic. Now it could abandon England's brutal punishment ways. It had an opportunity to design its own brand of "justice." In 1829, in Philadelphia, the first full-blown penitentiary opened.

Until this point, imprisonment had typically been a stage between crime and consequence: people were detained until their actual punishments were carried out. Public hanging, where people rushed to the gallows to watch the brutal spectacle, was popular. In Michel Foucault's 1975 book about the history and philosophy of Western punishment, *Discipline and Punish: The Birth of the Prison*, he paints a macabre picture of eighteenth-century France. After attempting to kill the king, a man is tortured in public and finally dismembered by horses. Foucault argues that this style of public punishment enforced the king's power. "The public execution did not re-establish justice; it re-activated power," Foucault writes. "Its ruthlessness, its spectacle, its physical violence, its unbalanced play of forces, its meticulous ceremonial, its entire apparatus were inscribed in the political functioning of the penal system."

These gruesome public scenes extended into the Age of Enlightenment. "Till the end of the eighteenth century, torture was normal investigative procedure in the Catholic church as well as in most European states," writes historian Arthur Schlesinger. However, reformers began to oppose these gothic methods. Among the political reformers was English philosopher Jeremy Bentham, an important advocate of social improvement. Bentham advocated for the abolition of slavery, the separation of church and state, and individual freedoms. (He is so revered a figure, particularly in England, that the University College London honored his wish to display his preserved corpse, as well as his separated head, in a clear box.) In 1787, Bentham visited his industrial-engineer brother, Samuel, in what is now Belarus, where Samuel had created a model for monitoring his workforce. Bentham believed he could mirror his brother's approach and create a specific institution for less brutal punishment: a civic building where wrongdoers could be morally rehabilitated. In 1791, Bentham teamed up with the architect Willey Reveley to create this new design: they called it the Panopticon.

Derived from the word *panoptic*, meaning "all-seeing," the Panopticon, Bentham argued, could encourage criminals to be better people. Consisting of tiers of cells wrapped around one tall guard tower, the Panopticon would give the guard on duty, in just one spin, full visual access to all those imprisoned. Theoretically, the paranoia of being caught doing something wrong would stop those locked inside from unruly behavior; as long as they felt they were being watched, they would behave. Foucault writes, "The panoptic mechanism arranges spatial unities that make it possible to see constantly and to recognize immediately. In short, it reverses the principle of the dungeon. . . . Visibility is a trap."

The Panopticon was never built in its intended form in England, but the concept managed to cross borders and was reproduced in other countries, such as Spain and the Netherlands. (In 1919, one large Panopticon-style prison was built in Statesville, Illinois.) Despite Bentham's approach never having been fully realized, the concept of an all-seeing authority inspired other thinkers and more societal outlooks to follow.

Another influential political reformer was Englishman John Howard, who visited prisons (essentially holding areas) around England and on the continent in the late eighteenth century.

He was shocked by the abysmal conditions, rampant diseases, and fees demanded of those imprisoned. "Jailers were not salaried but lived off fees paid by prisoners for food, bedding and other facilities. This system meant that poorer prisoners lived in terrible conditions. Many jailers demanded payment before prisoners were released, meaning that some stayed in jail even if they were innocent or had served their sentences," according to the BBC's historical archives. Howard advocated for a system of clean, state-run prisons. These new institutions could enforce solitary confinement, labor, and religious studies to help rehabilitate those inside, rather than simply punish them. Howard's advocacy helped lay the groundwork for a new concept about to be born in America.

In America, much of the European approach had remained intact. Public prisons had mainly served as holding pens, where 30 to 40 people would wait in these so-called "debauchery dens" until their time came to face their punishment. Steps were being taken to address abuses happening in these dens, and innately violent punishments. In Pennsylvania, Quaker beliefs rooted in silence, repentance, and rehabilitation led to the formation in 1787 of the Philadelphia Society for Alleviating the Miseries of Public Prisons. Its members included founding fathers Benjamin Franklin and Benjamin Rush, who was a correspondent of John Howard and adapted some of Howard's beliefs.

This Philadelphia reform group gathered at Ben Franklin's home, where Rush advocated for the benefits of solitude, working in isolation, and studying the Bible. The idea of penitence is intensely Christian, which appealed to the group. Devising a plan to abolish public flogging, disfigurement, and execution by the state, the group advocated for a formal, state-run institution to be built, where an experiment of rehabilitation could be carried out.

The state of Pennsylvania got on board, and in 1790 legislation was passed to renovate a local facility, Philadelphia's Walnut Street Jail, to add on a new cell house with 16 solitary cells. It would be a test run to see how this strategy of solitude would fare. Instead of sharing a common space, where violence and disease festered, some of the incarcerated would now live in solitary confinement, in cells measuring 6 feet by 8 feet by 9 feet, where they could pray and be redeemed.

This renovation, however, was not exactly what reformers had in mind. They imagined an entire civic institution dedicated to this experiment. For many years, the Philadelphia Society for Alleviating the Miseries of Public Prisons lobbied for a new style of institution. Finally, in 1821, the Pennsylvania legislature approved funding for what would be a new state-run institution. At the time, it was one of the most expensive buildings ever built in the country, costing $780,000—a harbinger of the nation's massive spending on prisons and jails to come.

The state launched a competition for architects to create a building that would embody this new system of correction. Young British architect John Haviland, who had settled in Philadelphia in 1816, submitted his plan. Haviland won the $100 prize for his Gothic design. The tall, imposing walls of this castle-like institution hid wrongdoers from public view. No longer would they be terrorized and humiliated in town and city centers; no longer would the people rush to the gallows. Inside, each incarcerated person would study the Bible, work, sleep, and eat in the solitude of his cell. This style of isolation became called the "Pennsylvania System." As Foucault writes in *Discipline and Punish*, "In the Pennsylvanian prison, the only operations of correction were the conscience and the silent architecture that confronted it." Haviland's structure was the first civic institution to try this large-scale moral experiment on involuntary subjects. When Eastern State Penitentiary opened in 1829, its revolutionary architecture set the tone for the future of punishment in the Western world.

The penitentiary, from the word *penitent*, was born.

Knowing how incarceration became America's main form of punishment is an important step in understanding today's criminal justice system. While Haviland's Eastern State Penitentiary no longer incarcerates people, it does offer guided tours. Intrigued to see "the flagship of American prison design," I drove toward Philadelphia, the last slice of Manhattan skyline fading in my rearview. Two hours later, I merged into the Saturday evening traffic on Fairmount Avenue, once a no-man's-land, now gentrified. As I drove past cafés and craft cocktail bars, Haviland's institution emerged, the bloodred sun casting a glow across this Gothic Revival masterpiece.

Built on former farmland known as Cherry Hill, the penitentiary was sealed off from the rest of society, its stone walls rising three stories high and descending ten feet underground, ensuring no one could escape. On October 25, 1829, Eastern opened, and prisoner number one was a Black man named Charles Williams. According to Eastern's history, Williams was in for charges of stealing a gold key and watch. From the start, this penitentiary held a disproportionate number of Black people, just as subsequent prisons and jails would. By winter of its first year, Eastern held 11 incarcerated people, and by the time Eastern closed in the 1970s, the prison had caged thousands more people than John Haviland had ever anticipated.

After the penitentiary closed, the city tried to sell the property for commercial real estate development, but a lively group of historic preservationists, community firebrands, and criminologists saved it from demolition. Refashioned as a nonprofit and a historic landmark, the building reopened in 1994, this time to the general public. As I approached the penitentiary, blackened moss crawled up its stone façade. The building seemed to warn, "Stay out."

I ventured in.

Standing sentry beneath the grand entranceway was an Eastern employee, to whom I explained I was here for the tour. With long, boney fingers, she handed me an MP3 player and headset. "Make sure you don't touch anything," she cautioned. "Don't want to bring any lead home with you." She motioned to an underground passage, and following her instruction, I headed down the dank tunnel.

When I emerged at the other end, I was inside the penitentiary walls. In the silvery twilight, a different world came into focus. Before me was Haviland's signature radial design, since copied by many architects for prisons and jails. From the center of the radius, the cell blocks fanned out in a circle like spokes on a wheel. This concept, partially inspired by the Panopticon's goal of constant surveillance, placed a guard in the middle who could stand and watch all the corridors in one spin. (In the Panopticon, the guard could see into the cells; at Eastern, the guard could see just the corridors.)

I put on the headset and pressed Play on the MP3 player. Actor and director Steve Buscemi greeted me, saying he'd be my guide for the audio tour. "You're standing inside the world's first true penitentiary, a building designed to inspire penitence—or true regret—in the hearts of criminals," Buscemi said. "The architects here believed that all human beings, regardless of their behavior, have good in their hearts. They believed Eastern State Penitentiary would inspire a new generation of prisons, worldwide, built on this optimism and faith in the human character. On the inside, Eastern State was progressive, even visionary."

I stepped into a cell block. Faded green paint peeled off the decaying walls, reminiscent of a 1970s horror movie scene in an insane asylum. The crumbling brick and stone of the tall, barrel-vaulted ceiling mimicked a haunted church. Ceiling skylights permitted squares of lavender light in the otherwise dark corridor. Buscemi said that when people were led to their cells, hoods were placed over their heads so they couldn't see the layout of the cells or see others inside them. Guards wore wool socks over their shoes to muffle sounds. The wardens' journals revealed that one individual who had disrupted the quiet was laced into a straitjacket and gagged; another was left in darkness, fed only bread and water.

Arranged along the cell block were small sliding doors that led to tomblike cells. Stepping inside, I felt a chill, despite the summer heat. At 8 feet by 12 feet, this dusty cell was large by today's standards—and dark, except for the narrow shaft of twilight coming through the deadeye* as if to suggest God is always watching. A Bible, a small bed, a workbench, and a cast-iron toilet were all that were allowed in the cell. (Eastern was, in fact, the first public building in America to have running-water toilets and a way of heating water for bathing—it had plumbing before the White House.) To prevent any talking, fighting, sexual activity, or disease from spreading, the cells were separated by 20-inch masonry walls. Three times a day, guards slid meals to the incarcerated people through a feeding hole in the cell door. Each person was forced to spend 23 hours a day in the cell, with one hour afforded for outdoor exercise. (A door in the back of each cell led to a walled-in, individual exercise space; Haviland believed, like many of his day, that diseases could be prevented with exposure to fresh air.)

What could be considered the first generation of modern prisons was born here. Solitary confinement quickly became the state's official policy for dealing with criminals. This method also provided a simple metric: time was measured in weeks, months, and years. The idea was that the length of the punishment would reflect the severity of the crime committed. After Eastern was erected, similar penitentiaries sprang up around the world, with the idea of imprisonment now widely accepted in the West. "The problem is the following," Foucault wrote in *Discipline and Punish*, "within a short space of time, detention became the essential

---

* John Haviland's small, conical skylight.

form of punishment. . . . It may be argued that it occurred almost instantaneously." Imprisonment was adopted as the modern method of punishment in the Western World.

Most visitors to Eastern State Penitentiary, including French sociologist and political theorist Alexis de Tocqueville, were highly positive regarding this new institution. This did not mean it did not have its critics, though. The English novelist Charles Dickens was staunchly against this grand experiment. Dickens, whose father had been locked up in a debtors' prison in England, saw the Pennsylvania System as cruel and ineffective. "In its intention I am well convinced that it is kind, humane, and meant for reformation; but I am persuaded that those who devised this system of Prison Discipline, and those benevolent gentlemen who carry it into execution, do not know what it is that they are doing," Dickens wrote in his travelogue, *American Notes for General Circulation.* "I believe that very few men are capable of estimating the immense amount of torture and agony that this dreadful punishment, prolonged for years, inflicts upon the sufferers. . . . I am only the more convinced that there is a depth of terrible endurance in it which none but the sufferers themselves can fathom, and which no man has a right to inflict upon his fellow-creature. I hold this slow and daily tampering with the mysteries of the brain to be immeasurably worse than any torture of the body . . . because its wounds are not upon the surface, and it extorts few cries that human ears can hear; therefore I the more denounce it, as a secret punishment which slumbering humanity is not roused up to stay." Those locked inside the building agreed. This extreme isolation and silence were far too severe, reports from some incarcerated people said. "In the gloomy solitude of a sullen cell, there is not one redeeming principle. There is but one step between the prisoner and insanity," said James Morton, who was incarcerated at Eastern.

Meanwhile, in New York State, another style of incarceration was being hatched. Here, incarcerated people were forced to work, building highways and roads, blacksmithing, or cobbling. Called the New York System, or the Auburn System, it had people working in groups, in silence, following a system that allegedly cultivated good work habits, encouraged mutual respect, and established paths to integrate people back into society: redemption found through hard work and militant organization and discipline. This philosophy aligned more with the values and incentives of the booming industrial revolution, with its forced labor and its stacked cells, providing a cost-efficient way to cage a large population. Foucault states this style was just another form of control by the state.

Over the next 50 years, debates ensued about which model was more effective—the Auburn System or the Pennsylvania System—with arguments ranging from the religious, medical, economic, and architectural to the administrative. Ultimately, the Auburn System triumphed in the United States because of the profits and low-cost labor it produced. (In the United States, there was a labor shortage, so prison labor was valued, rather than viewed as a threat; in Europe at this time, the Pennsylvania System was more common because of a different labor market, where prison labor would have threatened worker security.) That is, labor and money trumped redemption. Forced labor became a standard mode of punishment in these institutions; personal space was deemed a luxury, not to be wasted on a criminal. Architects designed rows upon rows of masonry cubes, stacked on top of one another, into which incarcerated people were crammed against their will. At Sing Sing, one of New York State's most infamous correctional facilities that still runs today, cells were built roughly the size of a coffin, only taller, at 7 feet deep, 3 feet 3 inches wide, and 6 feet 7 inches high. Many of Sing Sing's cells had no access to sunlight, fresh air, or views of the outdoors. Officials justified the conditions by saying that the cells were for sleeping only, since incarcerated people worked outside during the day.

In 1865, the United States abolished the institution of slavery, but a new form of slavery would ensue inside the nation's prisons and jails. Embedded in the Thirteenth Amendment was a menacing exception to slavery: "Neither slavery nor involuntary servitude, except as punishment for crime whereof the party shall have been duly convicted, shall exist within the United States, or any place subject to their jurisdiction." This clause allowed for slavery to be legal if someone broke the law. Before long, Black people became the targets of lawful surveillance and arrest, charged en masse for low-level crimes like loitering and vagrancy, then forced to work. During this period, prison labor was in such high demand that, in a remarkable affront to the end of legalized slave labor, prisons launched convict leasing programs, thereby keeping formerly enslaved people from obtaining the rights of ordinary workers.

In a perverse twist of history, some plantations were transformed into penitentiaries, such as Louisiana State Penitentiary. After the Civil War, former Confederate Major Samuel James leased imprisoned people from the state to work his land, Angola

Plantation, named after the African country where the plantation's formerly enslaved people came from. "In 1880, former Confederate Major Samuel James purchased the plantation and made it into a prison camp. . . . James converted the slave quarters into jail cells, but basically recreated slavery," according to *Prison-Insider*. In 1901, the state bought the land from the James family and incorporated Angola as a state prison. To this day, the Louisiana State Penitentiary is operated as a maximum-security prison farm and colloquially called "Angola."

The first paradigm shift to modern incarceration occurred when penitence was no longer the focus. Now the incarcerated would be forced to work, their rights eliminated, their privacy disregarded, their time no longer theirs. Oscar Wilde captures this feeling of despair in his poem "The Ballad of Reading Gaol," which he wrote about his own experience of prison:

> The vilest deeds, like poison weeds
> Bloom well in prison-air:
> It is only what is good in Man
> That wastes and withers there:
> Pale Anguish keeps the heavy gate,
> And the Warder is Despair.

Despite the hopelessness new prison architecture seemed to inflict, the U.S. was determined to build more prisons. In 1891, it established its federal prison system, with the first three federal penitentiaries as U.S. Penitentiary Leavenworth, in Kansas; U.S. Penitentiary Atlanta, in Georgia; and U.S. Penitentiary McNeil Island, in Washington state. As more federal prisons were built, there was a growing need for one supervising entity to oversee the nation's expanding prisons. In 1930, the Federal Bureau of Prisons was created to provide that centralized administration for all federal prisons. Four years later, the first maximum-security federal prison, Alcatraz, opened on an island near San Francisco, intended for caging only the most "incorrigible" people.

By the mid-twentieth century, Eastern State Penitentiary was deteriorating. Haviland's original design had been intended to hold only 250 people, but at its peak Eastern held 1,700. The incarcerated population far surpassed the number of people being released, which exacerbated overcrowding and hindered effective management, sanitation, and safety. Like many other first-generation prisons across America, this institution was difficult and expensive to run. Its plumbing was outdated. New wings were added to Eastern, corrupting Haviland's radial design. The need for natural ventilation and sunlight were ignored. Further, the cell blocks were segregated, as were the job assignments. Black people usually worked in the kitchen, while white people were given better choices, such as working in the print shop. By 1940, Eastern had become a maximum-security facility. In 1959, it added a death row. By this point, people here were serving life sentences, and some had been sentenced to death.

Around this time, applications of modern technology were accelerating. Several prisons started experimenting with CCTV (closed-circuit television). This surveillance system allowed for a new prison design, whereby people could be grouped in pods of 40 to 64 and could be under a camera's watchful eye, with guards behind Plexiglas barriers. This design style is called "indirect supervision" and could be considered the second generation of American prison design. While first-generation prisons could be said to have been inspired by goals of rehabilitation and moral rectitude, second-generation facilities were architectural solutions to problems of overcrowding and dangerous conditions.

In the 1960s, the state of Pennsylvania began the process of closing Eastern State Penitentiary, officially finishing the closure in 1970, as demands for change in the justice system grew around the nation. Incarcerated people were living in old, outdated prisons, with terrible ventilation, malfunctioning plumbing systems, and stuffed into cells with more people than should ever be allowed in one space.

After my audio tour with Steve Buscemi, I returned my audio player and walked the grounds.

"Hey!"

As I turned around, I noticed a young Eastern employee wearing a tie-dyed T-shirt, rainbow socks, and white patent-leather boots, who was trying to get my attention.

"Please go this way. Because over there," he nodded to a big white tent playing loud disco music, "we're having a bar mitzvah."

"You do bar mitzvahs here?"

"Oh, we have all kinds of things," said a young woman employee in ice cream cone–print pants, who'd ambled over to join us. "Birthdays, weddings, we even had an event for Monster. You know that energy drink?"

"People have their weddings at the penitentiary?" I confirmed.

"It's beautiful here!" the man said, spinning on the heel of his patent leather boot to take in a 360-degree view. "Why wouldn't you?"

"You can check out our beer garden, if you want," the woman offered, pointing to a grassy area decorated with picnic tables and a makeshift bar serving craft beers. I shook my head and kept walking, leaving behind the revelers as they tossed back brews under the crescent moon inside the prison walls.

So, Eastern had morphed into a wedding venue and a haunted house; some of the nation's older prisons had transmogrified into film settings, luxury hotels, or national parks. As I left Philadelphia, I thought about how much had changed since the Quakers and John Haviland had architected this building for redemption. When Eastern closed in 1970, America's era of mass incarceration was just beginning. For this growing number of prisons and jails, a massive crop of industries emerged, including a trade that became known as justice architecture.

THREE

The Justice Architects

Young *architect Gregory Cook* walked into the hotel just steps from the Mississippi River. It was a balmy fall day in 2014, and architects, sheriffs, judges, and administrators of departments of correction had traveled from across the nation for one of the most important events in the industry. "Justice architecture" is the lucrative niche dedicated to the design of prisons, jails, courthouses, and police stations.

Each year, a members-only group, the Academy of Architecture for Justice (AAJ)—a subgroup of the esteemed American Institute of Architects (AIA)—hosts this annual conference in a different city. This year, the Academy of Architecture for Justice Conference would be held in St. Louis, Missouri.

As the midwestern sun set, a judge welcomed guests with an opening-night speech. Guests then meandered onto the expo floor, where representatives in booths for about 40 companies awaited them, selling products such as precast concrete cells and steel furniture. The ArmorCore booth boasted its bullet-resistant fiberglass panels as "the cost-effective solution for designing bullet resistance into courtrooms, law enforcement and detention facilities, border patrol structures, and other projects." Chief Correctional Products sold steel cells and metal wall panels. Derby Industries introduced Derby STEEL, its new furniture line, including bunks and benches with built-in cuff slots.

Sponsoring the conference, as usual, was the illustrious architecture firm HOK, renowned for its sleek hotels, international airports, and museums, including the National Center for Civil and Human Rights, the Dalí Museum, InterContinental Beijing, LaGuardia airport's new terminal, and the Lotte New York Palace Hotel renovation. With 26 offices on 3 continents, the firm was one of the biggest players in the business. That year, HOK was cosponsoring the event with Safti First, a leading manufacturer of fire-rated glass that protects against attacks, blasts, and bullets.

Greg Cook was relatively new to the scene. Many of his peers had been in justice architecture for decades. Though Cook launched his career in justice architecture just several years before, he was already making his mark. As an employee of HOK, he began in commercial architecture and science and technology. In 2009, the global firm tasked Cook with his first major justice project: a maximum-security male prison in Iowa. Until this point, Cook honestly hadn't given much thought to America's criminal justice system. Like many Americans, he hadn't been affected by it. It wasn't until he went on a scouting visit to the prison that something stirred within him. "I never realized how many people there dedicate their lives to this very difficult work of helping other people get better," Cook recalled. "It was inspiring, to be perfectly honest. The staff were talented, smart, and deeply committed to doing what's right."

The architect spoke with the prison's staff members and listened to their concerns. Many said the physical environment was the most significant impediment to their work. Cook was moved. "As an architect, if you have an opportunity to work with a client who wants to improve the lives of the people who are held in a facility, and who work in a facility, I think that's a really noble thing to take on," Cook told me. "And I think we have a lot to contribute." He believed he could help improve their work and their success through design. Cook modeled the new Iowa prison after a community-college campus with residential units, believing it was important for incarcerated people to have a level of personal control, where they could manage their own schedules and roam more freely, "rather than being herded around by a correction officer."

In 2010, Cook took his investment in justice architecture a step further: he became the nation's first architect to be certified as a correctional health professional. This knowledge, he believed, was crucial for designing supportive environments where people could rehabilitate. Cook remembered his peers, including nurses, social workers, and psychologists who worked in detention settings, being shocked to see an architect interested in correctional health. "They looked at me like I was from Mars," he told me.

As Cook was tasked with more jail and prison design projects, the field of justice architecture was experiencing a shift. By 2014, when Cook attended the St. Louis conference, the industry had integrated themes of equity and more humane conditions. Fittingly, the 2014 conference in St. Louis was called "Architecture for Social Justice." This year, Cook was being celebrated as one of the "emerging professionals." His Iowa State Penitentiary project was one of the prisons awarded at the conference's annual award show, since it was "impressive for a state penitentiary—great concept and integration into the region," the Justice Facilities Review proclaimed.

Cook differed from some of his peers. The young architect possessed a certain optimism that design could help address some of the most brutal parts of America's criminal justice system. His ethos was grounded in the belief that the design approach should focus on the needs of those living and working in detention.

Other justice architects, some of an older guard, seemed more reluctant to change.

To know more about the power players and philosophies of justice architecture, I first sought out the history of this trade. There is little public information about this industry and its most dedicated groups. It's unclear whether this information is hidden or is just extremely niche.

I studied the websites and marketing materials of justice architecture firms, ranging from mom-and-pop shops to global corporations. While some of the smaller shops declare their status as justice firms, displaying multiple detention projects online, some of the international firms obfuscate their work in the field. Some of justice architecture's biggest players, like HOK and HDR, have designed hundreds of justice facilities. Yet many of these projects are absent from their portfolios. On HOK's website, under a small tab marked "Justice," only four of HOK's justice projects were listed, mainly courthouses. However, HOK has designed far more than four justice projects. HDR, too, notes only a small number of its justice projects on its website. Under a tab marked "Civic," it lists only nine projects, placing an emphasis on "using the design process to promote meaningful restorative justice and human dignity." As of 2021, this multibillion-dollar firm designed over 275 jails and prisons.

Some believe this mystification is because the concept of detention settings clashes with the glimmering aesthetics desired by more glamorous clients. Another standpoint is that it's designed to be opaque because of the nature of the field itself. "You're going to find a lot of courthouses because they look beautiful and great on the screen," Cook told me. "You'll find some correctional facilities, but you're not going to find all of them. That's a select few of their projects that they put up. There's a lot of work that happens that no one ever sees, and it tends to be the stuff that's not very progressive in nature."

I visited the New York Public Library to comb through any archived materials about justice architecture, the AAJ, or the history of American prison and jail design in general. To the librarian's shock, and mine as well, there was little information. I sought out trade books, white papers, and notes. I reached out to the AIA to get more info on the AAJ and its history. All the AIA staff member could find, he explained, was a brief timeline. I pressed further. Eventually, the employee emailed me meeting notes that dated from the 1970s. These notes revealed crucial information. Paired with on- and off-the-record interviews of veterans in and around the business, I was able to piece together a more comprehensive history.

The AAJ's earliest iteration, as best can be discerned, was

formed in the early 1970s, under the name of the Task Force on Correctional Architecture. The national atmosphere was tense and tumultuous; in 1968, Martin Luther King Jr. was assassinated, race riots and protests rose in many cities, and many people were irate about involvement in Vietnam. New York City was plunged into an economic decline and suffered a great deal of violence. Outdated prisons and jails were overpopulated with a disproportionate number of Black and Brown people. Those inside the prisons tried to make those abysmal conditions public knowledge. In 1971, incarcerated people rioted for five straight days during the Attica Prison Massacre, demanding better conditions and more rights. It was the most fatal prison uprising in American history (33 incarcerated men and 10 staff members died). Around this same time, many of the nation's older jails and prisons—some still operating from the nineteenth century—were crumbling, with unsanitary living conditions. People around the country demanded the government improve its prisons and jails. Some wanted these institutions closed—for good. The country was pulsing with outrage and revolution.

The U.S. government launched task forces and committees to evaluate the current criminal justice system and the outdated architecture of its institutions. Congress passed the Omnibus Crime Control and Safe Streets Act of 1968, which provided federal funds to build new jails and prisons around the country. The Department of Justice would issue the federal funds through its new agency, the Law Enforcement Assistance Administration (LEAA). There was a catch: those seeking these federal funds would have to comply with "advanced practices" in their jail and prison designs.

Enter the National Clearinghouse for Criminal Justice Planning and Architecture.

In 1971, the LEAA issued a request for proposals for developing what these "advanced practices" in correctional facility design would be. A team from the University of Illinois, led by Professor of Architecture Fred Moyer—whose work had an important impact on this field—proposed a "total systems approach," which included incarceration alternatives. After getting the sign-off, this small but mighty team—now funded by the LEAA—took shape as a new organization, the National Clearinghouse for Criminal Justice Planning and Architecture. Those wanting to clench federal funds would have to abide by the Clearinghouse's new design principles, including "unobtrusive security" and "normalized" housing and programs.

Over time, the Clearinghouse grew to more than one hundred professionals, including architects, planners, social scientists, law enforcement officials, and attorneys. They reviewed over 3,000 plans, accompanied by a program of technical assistance. The Clearinghouse advocated for alternatives to incarceration within the community, with facilities on an as-needed basis. While this federal subsidization of prisons and jails was ostensibly to achieve an improved justice system, what followed was the era of mass incarceration, during which millions of people were locked up in numbers the world had not seen before.

Throughout this time, the AIA was paying close attention from its headquarters in Washington, D.C. Founded in 1857, the members-only organization now comprises over 200 chapters. According to its website, its goal is to advocate for "public policies that promote economic vitality and public wellbeing." As the voice of architects in America, the AIA surely understood that architects would play a fundamental role in the future of America's prisons and jails. In 1972, what could be considered the AAJ's predecessor was formed under the AIA. Named the Task Force on Correctional Architecture, it attracted architects who had previously designed facilities, as well as architects looking to get involved in the field. Leader of the Clearinghouse Fred Moyer was invited to be an original member, and he helped interface between the Clearinghouse and the AIA's new task force.

In its nascent stages, the task force held that America's prisons and jails were unacceptable. "The confinement of man in barred cages for detention is not correctional and no longer considered humane or within the framework of human dignity," said the task force's meeting notes from 1972. These architects weren't just interested in changing how these justice settings operated; they also wanted to change how architects operated. In the past, many architects had seemed more concerned with meeting their clients' needs, "selling their concept of security by 'caging' without understanding or recognizing the more deeply rooted problems of corrections," the meeting notes stated. This needed to change, the task force agreed. Fresh ideas had to be exchanged and new methods employed.

In 1974, the task force held its inaugural conference in Kansas City, Missouri. The conference aimed to "explore new concepts of correctional systems and the role of the architect in programming and design to bring about change in the correctional environment," the task force said. More architects became interested in this field. By 1975, the Task Force on Correctional Architecture had grown to 52 members and continued to grow, despite the eventual shuttering of the Clearinghouse during the Carter Administration. The group went through multiple iterations and names, until 2005, when it emerged as its current iteration: the Academy of Architecture for Justice.

Today, the AAJ has 2,300 members.

As the field of justice architecture flourished, America experienced a seismic jail and prison construction boom. *Los Angeles Times* architecture critic Christopher Hawthorne said, "it might be the most carefully hidden building boom in American architectural history." Major political forces were at play. From the White House, President Richard Nixon launched his "War on Drugs" in 1971. Ten years later, President Ronald Reagan continued Nixon's efforts through his policies focused on crime and welfare. Drug use, drug sales, and addiction were deemed criminal issues, rather than a public health crisis. Scores of people—a disproportionate number of whom were people of color—were locked up for marijuana, heroin, crack, and other drug offenses, and were demonized by the corporate media and tough-on-crime politicians. Some say these policies directly benefited the justice firms tasked with supplying demand. Justice architect Frank Greene, who started a justice architecture practice in 1989, saw it firsthand: "There was a whole type of architect and company, including private companies, who wanted to bang this stuff out like sausage, where no one cared about the impact on people who were being incarcerated."

Later, in the 2000s, public sentiment showed a renewed

interest in a more humane criminal justice system. Some noticed the justice architecture community adopting a softer, kinder tone, opting for more progressive rhetoric. "Those architects can't really get work anymore; no one is buying that way anymore," Greene said. "For many years, political discourse made hay out of demonizing racial minorities, they were treated as monsters . . . instead of recognizing traumas that led to this." Justice architecture conferences started integrating themes of social justice and inclusivity, such as the 2014 conference in St. Louis where Greg Cook was being honored. Reformers and advocates were asked to speak on panel discussions. The program's cover featured the faces of historical Black figures, such as Maya Angelou, Dred Scott, and Josephine Baker.* There remained, however, a major discrepancy in Black representation in the architecture field. Of all the nation's licensed architects, fewer than 3 percent are Black. Despite the change in pitch, there are lingering issues in the architecture community. As Greg Cook said, "The rhetoric changed, but the architecture is still catching up."

———

In early 2020, justice architects were gearing up for New York City's Borough-Based Jails (BBJ) program. On February 4, 2020, the city agency spearheading the design for the program, the Department of Design and Construction (DDC), launched

———

* Who are also considered St. Louis icons.

its request for qualifications. Architecture firms interested in bidding on the new jails could now submit their qualifications to the city. Each jail was a massive undertaking, and each firm could submit for only one jail.

For the first time, the city could use the design-build method, allowing for a more creative and efficient way to build. Thanks to new legislation passed in 2019, New York City could use the design-build delivery method, allowing it to work in a unified way, led by one single point of contact responsible for both design and construction. Design-build teams, consisting of both an architecture firm and a construction firm, would submit their proposals together. Previously, the city was required to award projects to the lowest bidder,* which reportedly caused long delays, costing a fortune. Another plus with design-build was that construction could begin while the jails were still being designed, which could save costs, time, and power struggles. Many eyes were on the BBJ program, partially because it would be the city's first design-build project out of the chute.

Because of the BBJ program's sheer scale, the DDC couldn't manage the process alone. The agency awarded a $107.4 million contract to AECOM-Hill, a joint undertaking of two massive consulting firms, AECOM and Hill International, to help manage the program. AECOM, a Fortune 500 giant, raked in about $20.2 billion in 2019 alone, and seemed like an exemplary partner: they'd worked on the Twin Towers, One World Trade

---

* As long as they met the qualifications.

Center, Atlanta's Mercedes-Benz Stadium, and hundreds of justice projects. Together with construction firm Hill International, they'd structure the procurement, manage each design-build team, and develop the requirements.

The architecture of the new Borough-Based Jails would need to be cutting edge, using the best of the best in justice architecture. Using softer materials, better lighting, and ample programming space, the city touted the Borough-Based Jails as a setting for rehabilitation. All four jails were to be "beacons of high-quality civic architecture that integrate into the immediate neighborhood context and are assets to all New Yorkers," the design guidelines declared, "grounded in dignity and respect." Each jail had its own specific guidelines. The Manhattan-based jail needed to integrate 20,000 square feet of "community and commercial space" on its ground level, and the arcade should be "inviting and hospitable to pedestrians." The Brooklyn jail's "ground floor facades should enliven the sidewalk experience." The jails needed to allow sunlight, programming space, and greenery.

In addition, each jail was required to use the direct-supervision model, as opposed to the indirect-supervision model, which is used at places like Rikers Island. Indirect supervision presupposes incarcerated people—many are untried—are dangerous and the staff must be protected. Thus, this model relies on technology, steel bars, and remote monitoring. The philosophy of direct supervision invests in the belief that design affects behavior. If someone is put in a cage, they'll act like an animal. Thus, direct supervision pairs a better living environment with kinder, direct interactions with staff, theoretically creating a safer, calmer setting. When people are incarcerated in a direct-supervision facility, they are classified according to their needs and assigned necessary treatments, programs, and living situations. Direct supervision lacks the typical hard barriers of a detention setting, such as bulletproof glass and steel bars. In a direct-supervision environment, one unarmed correction officer mans an open dorm unit with 70 to 80 incarcerated people. This is where the correction officer (CO) is to work, handle paperwork, and communicate in a helpful way. To keep the peace, direct supervision relies heavily on a reward-and-punishment system. Good behavior grants more freedoms, such as access to main corridors and attending programs.

This behavioral approach is supported by the actual architecture of the facility: residential pods with cells are arranged around the dayrooms; softer materials like wood and plastic replace the steel and concrete in furnishings; and access to natural light and some kind of outdoor recreation, like a basketball court, is viewed as basic necessities. Noninstitutional colors, like blue and green, are preferred, which is said to encourage better behavior and reduce vandalism. According to the Lippman report, evidence suggests that direct supervision can stave off violence if the staff is trained well, incarcerated people are classified correctly, and the leadership is well implemented.

"It is hard for someone who has not seen these [direct-supervision] jails and their contemporaries to understand how truly revolutionary they were then and remain today. Visually and operationally, they were light-years apart from other jails anywhere," wrote psychologist Dr. Richard Wener, who studied the effects of correctional architecture on incarcerated people and staff, in his seminal book *The Environmental Psychology of Prisons and Jails.*

When the concept of direct supervision first launched in 1974 by the U.S. Bureau of Prisons, it was controversial. When the first three direct-supervision prisons were built, some experienced professionals believed this new model was doomed to fail. Critics demanded to know how a correction officer could survive unarmed in a room filled with incarcerated people. There were also supporters who saw great value in the direct-supervision model. Some believed that if you put someone in a cage, that person will act like someone in a cage. Others believed the pretrial detainees in the nation's jails are innocent until proven guilty and should be treated with dignity and respect. Some argued that it wasn't about treatment—it was about upkeep and progress. "Not only were conditions deteriorated and functionally obsolete, but they did not enjoy the status of being considered architecture," Fred Moyer, head of the Clearinghouse, told *Correctional News* in a 2012 interview. "There was little respect for the humanity of the people who lived and worked in them. I have spent the past 42 years trying to change that picture." Over the last several decades, justice architects began adopting direct supervision to more designs. Today it's widely recognized by the industry as the best style of management and design.

Justice architect Greg Cook said one of the most rewarding projects of his career was a direct-supervision jail. Located in Hot Springs, Arkansas, the jail had been built as a result of the old jail being outdated and overpopulated. Many hoped a new jail with a better setting could help rehabilitate incarcerated people and set them on a better path. HOK won the bid to design Hot Springs's new Garland County Detention Center, and Cook started working on the plans. In 2015, when the architect visited the completed direct-supervision jail, he had a profound experience. A lobby receptionist told Cook to head inside the jail without an officer. "It really challenged my beliefs. . . . I never believed I could go in unescorted. . . . I walked down the main corridor, which all of the incarcerated people have access to. It really made me practice what I preach." The architect was pleasantly surprised to find he didn't feel in danger or threatened. The environment actually felt inspiring. He relished the simplicity of the direct-supervision approach. "There's nothing about that building that's overly designed," Cook said. "It's a very simple idea that was centered on creating an environment that was full of natural light, allowed for meaningful engagement between inmates and officers, and by creating an environment where you can have meaningful conversation and build trust, you can support the rehabilitation of the inmate because you're reducing stress, promoting pro-social behavior, and I think you create a pathway for rehabilitation that's otherwise not there."

When I again spoke with Cook, he'd since left HOK and was working for HDR. Since he'd first started in justice architecture, Cook had gained valuable insights. He spoke on panel discussions, such as "Pay It Forward—It's Our Professional Duty: The Next Generation of Justice Leadership" and "Positive Trends: How New Design Approaches are Improving Outcomes." In 2020, he served as chair of the Academy of Architecture for Justice. When

I asked Cook about his feelings on New York City's decision to close Rikers and build new jails, he replied, "I think it's the right move, absolutely. The population is down, so the timing is right. And it supports a new way of thinking. . . . It's such a big city, it's hard to have one mega facility. . . . They should be thinking about keeping the services close and where their families live. Keep them as close as possible."

Incarcerated people, like Moose, felt differently.

FOUR

The Incarcerated

H*ey. What's going on?"*
The deep baritone voice crackled through the phone, immediately recognizable.

"They transferred me to The Boat," Moose sighed, referring to the Vernon C. Bain Correctional Center, a floating jail that rests in the East River, just off the southern shore of the South Bronx. As part of the BBJ program, this jail was slated to close and a new high-rise jail was expected to be built on land nearby. The Boat was a far cry from the Gothic Revival architecture of Eastern State Penitentiary, a reminder of how far we've taken the punishment of incarceration. This giant barge has rested here since the early 1990s, when then New York City mayor Edward Koch determined floating jails could be the way of the future. Around this time, most of New York City's 21,800 jail beds were filled. Floating jails, the idea went, could use space that wouldn't be otherwise used, complained about, or missed during a period of severe jail overcrowding. $161 million was spent to build The Boat outside of New Orleans and transport it to New York, where it joined a fleet of four other maritime jails. Able to hold

800 incarcerated people and 317 workers, it has a yearly operational cost of nearly $24 million.

Every night, Moose fell asleep on a thin mattress, the black winds howling across the inky waters. Surrounded by razor wire, the postapocalyptic-like barge lives off an industrial peninsula called Hunts Point. To reach The Boat, one navigates past an army of semitrucks, active construction sites, and junked-car depots, the pungent smell of fish wafting from wholesale markets through the wide, uneven streets. The sounds of diesel trucks and seagulls fill the air, but once at The Boat, it seems eerily silent—at least from the outside.

Inside, conditions were bleak, but Moose wasn't complaining. As someone who'd been in and out of detention for nearly 20 years, Moose knew the system and had acquired a canny understanding of life inside. Over the last few months alone, he'd been locked up at Rikers, the Tombs, and The Boat. In the wayward logic of this world, he was part of the establishment, integral to this system that has its own ways of operating, its own style of politics, its own argot. Here, everything is turned upside down. Officially, wardens and COs rule, but the incarcerated have their modus operandi for these harsh, artificial settings: they create this code and pass it on to new fish. It was here that Moose commanded respect. Even people who'd never met Moose had heard of Moose.

"How's your arm?" I asked.

"They finally gave me wound care for the gunshot. I have screws in my arm now, but I still feel a sharp pain where the bullet was lodged."

"Sorry to hear that. Glad they took care of it."

"The days just languish here. At least at the Tombs they have cable. At Rikers, there's three TVs in a unit. There's never a dull moment at Rikers Island. Here, I just watch people on jet skis."

I broached the BBJ program again, to understand why he was against it. "Why not just take the time to fix it [Rikers] up?" he posed, echoing more conservative viewpoints, including that of Manhattan Institute for Policy Research senior fellow Nicole Gelinas, who felt that reimagining Rikers Island as a modern jail complex would be a better alternative to the Borough-Based Jails program. "If you're going to build new buildings in the boroughs and paint the walls a different color, that won't make a difference."

Moose was convinced that the new jails would be a waste of money, and they certainly wouldn't guarantee better conditions or care. There was flat, open land on Rikers, Moose said, that could be used for therapeutic outdoor space, art classes, and places for autonomy. Any movements of people locked up in the new high-rise jails would be limited to the staircases and elevators. That is, if they could leave their floor at all.

"Even if they want to close the jails and turn the land into a habitable neighborhood—build apartments or nightclubs—it has a smell; there's a huge rat population, and it's so close to the airport," Moose said. "You couldn't get much for rent."

Just fix up Rikers, he continued. "The way Rikers is designed now is physically disciplinary. The environment itself punishes the people inside. . . . Give us internet, carpets, make it more progressive," Moose said. "In Oslo, even child molesters and rapists get a couch and air conditioning. It's all about rehabilitation."

Changing locations and jail settings would do nothing to

change the innate hierarchies inside the jails, Moose said. To Moose, security and gang intelligence—the units that aim to prevent gang violence in specific areas—needed to be the first priorities in detention settings. Any belief that these intricate systems and relationships could be dismantled, he insisted, was futile.

Gangs in particular have presented major obstacles in correction settings, even to running the day-to-day life in the jails and prisons. New York City has had street gangs for over a century. In the 1980s, the city saw its first major gang organized inside a jail. Around this time, the incarcerated populations were becoming more diverse and more unpredictable, and so people were banding together—usually by ethnic background—for solidarity and protection. These groups became well organized—bureaucratic, even—with their own relationships, strategies, and business development plans. The way Moose saw it, the gangs would always run the jails. "They're wolf packs. There's one leader, and when he fails, another one steps up."

Solitary confinement, Moose believed, was also necessary, though this is a controversial stance. To many justice advocates and mental health experts, solitary confinement is viewed as cruel and unusual punishment. The practice is widely discussed as a human rights issue. The United Nations deemed any solitary confinement over 15 consecutive days to be torture. A 2019 study by the *Journal of the American Medical Association* found that people who are forced into solitary are 78 percent more likely to commit suicide. That was the case for Kalief Browder: shortly after being released from Rikers after spending three years in pretrial detention—two of which were spent in solitary—he took his own life. Rapper Lil Wayne, who was locked in solitary on Rikers after being caught with headphones and an MP3 charger, said it was the closest he'd ever come to killing himself.

Moose, however, was adamant. "They need to keep one building—a tall building, 10 to 15 floors—for solitary confinement, for the really violent criminals, for the people who really just don't give a shit." Because as far as Moose was concerned, there'd always be people who don't give a shit. His belief in solitary was aligned with the opinions of some correctional staff, who consider solitary an invaluable tool. Violence, according to Moose, would always be part of the incarceration experience, but solitary could separate the gang members and isolate the mentally ill people from the general jail population.

The only part of the city's Borough-Based Jails plan Moose seemed in favor of was the city's promise of ample programming space. Throughout the years he'd spent behind bars, Moose had earned 14 certifications. "I'm a Sagittarius, so I start things and don't finish them. I get bored easily. I need challenges," he explained. Moose was a major advocate of programs—so much so that he'd championed support and participation for the Rikers Debate Project, where he and his peers jousted in Parliamentary-style debates. At times, the incarcerated students went up against Ivy League teams. Every week, Rikers Debate held court in a cinderblock classroom fitted with old chairs, used books, and windows with rusted bars. Moose led debates and recruited others to join. He whipped the class into shape, challenging them to think outside the box and ask questions. He was a motivator, an intellectual, and a fantastic orator, according to the Rikers Debate volunteers, known for brightening up a room with his big-bellied laugh and bright smile. When Moose cared about something, everyone else cared about it, too. He was teacher's pet and life of the party.

"The only way to find salvation is to be authentic," Moose preached. If jails offered more programs, they could open up people's minds, beyond learning how to be better criminals, he said. Helping them focus on other subjects and earn degrees wouldn't just help them; it would also help society as a whole. New York City could take credit for that transformation. "[The city] can literally brainwash them into being smarter men—get them degrees. They can come out scholars and actually come home and get careers. It could be an investment, not a black hole."

It can be difficult to grasp the black hole that is jail—unless you've been inside. Stanley Richards understands. Richards was incarcerated at Rikers in the 1980s for two and a half years. He was one of the many Black man locked up. Even though Black people represent 13.6 percent of the U.S. population, one in three Black men will be sentenced to prison. For Latino men, it's one in every six. For white men, it's one in 17.

After getting released from Rikers Island, Richards was able to find a job at a New York City nonprofit, the Fortune Society, working as a counselor, where he helped people transition back to the Free World. In 2014, the Obama administration recognized Richards as a "Champion of Change." Richards was also influential in the BBJ program, sitting on the subcommittee on design of the Implementation Task Force. Today he serves as the executive vice president of the Fortune Society and sits on the board of the New York City Department of Correction. By many measures, Richards was the exception.

"People tell us, 'You'll never amount to anything—you'll end up in jail, prison, or the cemetery,'" Richards told me. "Teachers, the media and how it presents us, people you interact with on the streets, the people who have access to power. As a young Black boy, a Black teen, and a man, all the messages [you receive] and experiences you have communicate [the message that] your life doesn't matter."

Discriminatory practices and policies have infiltrated American society, from Reconstruction, to segregation, to the civil rights movement, to the crack epidemic, to the murder of George Floyd. Following the launch of the "war on drugs" in the early 1970s, America's incarcerated population grew exponentially until the mid-1990s (then started declining in the aughts). Michelle Alexander reported in her pivotal book, *The New Jim Crow*, that "mass incarceration in the United States had, in fact, emerged as a stunningly comprehensive and well-disguised system of racialized social control that functions in a manner strikingly similar to Jim Crow." One example of this racist legislation was designed around crack cocaine, the annihilative white rocks whose prevalence tore through some of America's poorest neighborhoods. American officials chose to categorize crack cocaine as a criminal issue, and established long sentences for crack-cocaine convictions, ballooning the populations in jails and prisons.

This kind of discrimination is exacerbated by the fact that Black and Brown communities have systemically been denied access to good schools, community programs, clean parks and sports fields, good libraries, and adequate healthcare. The priorities are skewed. For instance, while New York City spends $400 million a year on its libraries, it dropped $421 million on one courthouse in the Bronx. The courthouse, designed by starchitect Rafael Viñoly, is larger* than its neighbor Yankee Stadium. Where the city's funds go, how its facilities are designed, and how they are maintained (or ignored) reflects the society's priorities. In many ways, these factors work in concert against poorer neighborhoods, leaving locals with few options. As the child of an incarcerated parent once told me, "You either gotta play ball or rap to get out."

With its BBJ program, New York City seemed determined to use the new jails to help prepare the incarcerated for success upon their release. When I asked Stanley Richards if he thought the new jail designs could help change things, he replied, "Design is a facilitator, but it's not a sustainer. Sustaining comes from cultural change." I told him about Moose's stance, and Richards understood Moose's paradoxical position. Richards saw how one could become so accustomed to the jail surroundings that no matter how traumatic they are, a person adjusts to them. The situation becomes normalized. Humans are so adaptable that even ugly circumstances can be accepted—when there seems to be no other choice. Richards offered a metaphor: "A fish in a fishbowl with cloudy water adapts to that water and learns how to swim and live. But then, another fish comes into the water and says, 'Oh, my gosh, why is it so dirty and cloudy in here?' The fish that's been in there awhile doesn't see that it's murky." Moose had

---

* By square footage.

been in the system for most of his adult life; this was his world. To change that world could be seismic, nearly impossible. Richards added, "Some of the smartest and brightest and most creative people are locked in cages."

———

Where Moose and Richards agree is that education and programs can help people change, and the data support this. Also crucial is receiving support once released. This support can come in the form of housing, jobs, therapy, religious or spiritual practices, anger management, addiction programs, and stronger connections to family and friends. So often, while people are locked up, they don't have access to these lifelines. Once outside, this support can be crucial in saving lives and reducing the likelihood of going back into jail.

In the first two weeks of release, parolees have a death rate that is 13 times higher than anyone else in their demographic who hasn't been incarcerated. The first 72 hours after someone is released are critical. According to a report by the Stanford Criminal Justice Center, recent parolees need to be connected to safe environments, receive counseling, get access to jobs, have contact with loved ones, and receive other forms of support—all to help with a successful reentry into the Free World. In theory, there are many nonprofits and government groups that seek to be of assistance. On the ground, there can be few options and little help. As Richards said, some of jails' most powerful players are later seen on the streets, pushing grocery carts with all their belongings.

The lives of the newly released are often no longer the same as before their incarceration. Their former relationships, jobs, living situations, social networks, and other support structures can vanish. When a person has been cut off from society, locked up on a carceral island or on a barge, placed on a former plantation, or hidden inside a fortress, that person's life can be frozen in time; the rest of the world has left the individual behind. When released, the person can face extreme difficulty in finding a job, securing housing, or obtaining healthcare—not to mention receiving support for the trauma and emotional damage caused by that recent incarceration. With no place to live independently, they may become reimmersed in the structural mire that led them to jail in the first place. Perversely, the Free World can be so cold and alienating that return to jail may not feel like the worst option.

When Moose wasn't locked up, he typically couch-surfed at his friends' places or crashed with his mom, who was a field nurse. Shelters, he vowed, were out of the question. Many others feel the same, refusing to check in owing to their often unsafe, unsanitary conditions. In the last 40 years, the number of shelter beds in New York City grew from 3,600 to a system that sleeps 56,000 per night. Still, there often aren't enough beds. Upon entering, people may find some of these shelters reminiscent of a detention environment. The entry has metal detectors and police from the Department of Homeless Services. After "the client" gives basic information to the staff, the client navigates this massive place alone, finding his bed in large open dorms that typically sleep at least 20 people. The smell of synthetic cannabis, K2, seeps through the corridors. The bathrooms are often disgusting. Though lockers are provided for a few personal belongings, theft is common. Rodents make their nests in the beds and cockroaches crawl through the rationed food. Further, residents often don't sleep in the same bed—or even the same shelter—each night. Everyone is awoken at the crack of dawn, forced to leave the shelter for most of the day, with a tight curfew of 11 p.m. With little consistency in their lives, they are often moved from shelter to shelter, which could be in any of the city's five boroughs, and they never know where they'll sleep each night. The majority of people who live in the shelters have at least one disability, with higher rates of mental illness, addiction issues, and other severe health problems. This population overload, plus a lack of services, means that the shelters can be scary and anarchic, compounded by hard drug use and physical threats. Some people brave the city streets and sleep in public spaces, like Penn Station and the Port Authority, or in the subway. In the early 2020s, New York City's homelessness rate is the highest it's been since the Great Depression. It is only part of a larger nationwide rise in homelessness.

While homelessness is a complicated issue with myriad causes, the number one reason for homelessness is a lack of affordable housing. In New York City, the availability of rentals under $1,500 a month is less than 1 percent. In a healthy market, the number of housing opportunities should coincide with the number of people looking for a spot to live. Nationwide, housing production was lacking by 7.3 million homes (from 2000 to 2015). Without consistent shelter, a whole other slew of issues can emerge.

For example, those who live on the street are way more likely to have run-ins with the police. On average, they have 21 contacts over a course of six months (measured between 2015 and 2017), according to the California Policy Lab, as cited in "Five Charts That Explain the Homelessness-Jail Cycle—and How to Break It." The likelihood of getting arrested for low-level crimes, like loitering or public urination, becomes far greater. Situations can escalate unnecessarily, resulting in higher-level conflicts and consequences. Because of this lack of housing and support resources, the public's response to homelessness can be to call the police. The cycle continues: unhoused individuals often can't afford bail, and thus are tossed in jail. One report out of Los Angeles found that in Los Angeles alone, people experiencing homelessness accounted for $79.6 million of the arrests and jail stays in the 2014–15 fiscal year. In Connecticut, a study found that 69 percent of incarcerated people had previously lacked a place to live. Meanwhile, in New York State, a NY1 investigation found that over half of the people paroled from state prisons in 2017 went to shelters (run by the Department of Homeless Services; this doesn't count shelters run by nonprofits, like Exodus or the Fortune Society, or those who slept on the streets); this is the cycle of poverty, homelessness, and incarceration that persists.

In the past, incarceration and homelessness have been perceived as mainly a male problem. In recent years, a better understanding has emerged, seeing these issues as gender neutral. Nationwide, men overwhelming account for the incarcerated population (90 percent), but in the last 25 years there has been a surge in the women's population. That is, it was nearly five times higher in 2020 than in 1980 (twice as great as male growth in population), with 1 million women under the supervision of the U.S. criminal justice system.

Camilla Broderick was a young woman incarcerated on

Rikers from September 2016 through May 2017 because of an addiction to opioids. As a teenager, she started using them to help cope with depression. When Broderick was in her early twenties, an undercover cop posed as an addict on Craigslist and asked her to sell him a $10 bag of dope and a few pills. Broderick met up with the cop in downtown Manhattan, close to her parents' apartment building. After the exchange, the cop waited until she entered her building, then several officers nabbed her.

Drugs are a big driver of incarceration rates. Jails are on the front lines of the nation's opioid crisis, with at least a fourth of the incarcerated population suffering from opioid addiction. An extensive study conducted by Columbia University found that 80 percent of the nation's incarcerated population was seriously involved in substance use. A woman attorney incarcerated in a New Jersey jail for her third DUI told me that although she'd been doing Alcoholics Anonymous outside of jail, there were no addiction programs for her and her peers once inside. All that was accessible, she said, was drugs—mainly fentanyl. These drugs come at a high premium inside—costing far more than street drugs—typically arriving through gang members, correction officers, or the mail. Mental health professional Mary Buser, who worked on Rikers for five years, told me that virtually everyone inside Rikers had a drug issue. "I can think of [only] five people who didn't, and I worked with hundreds of people," she said. "All roads lead to drugs. Everything was drugs, drugs, drugs."

Some offenders, like Camilla Broderick, are given a chance. After her arrest downtown, Broderick was handed a judge-ordered 18-month rehab program. For others, especially those of color, jail is the first stop. (A California-based study found Black and Hispanic people are significantly more likely to be incarcerated and less likely to receive a diversion to drug treatment than white people.) Broderick didn't get sober the first time around. After failing the 18-month rehab in 90 days, she was rerouted to Rikers Island.

The Rose M. Singer Center, or "Rosie's," as it is called, is the pink women's jail on Rikers. Here, most women have issues with substance abuse and almost all have suffered trauma and violence. Many are mothers. In the nation's prisons, half the women typically are mothers; in jails, 80 percent are moms. In 2017, two-thirds reported that they were struggling with mental illness. When Broderick entered Rosie's, she was terrified. Leading up to her incarceration, she had watched multiple episodes of the Netflix series *Locked Up*, which primed her for the harsh and dangerous conditions of detention. Broderick was convinced that, as a white woman, she would be attacked. She was put on suicide watch for the first 24 hours, which she said was humiliating.

While some facilities may offer 90-day rehab programs, many do not. People like Broderick are left to detox on their own. By the most basic standards, jail facilities are not proper detox centers. Sobering up often requires a level of vulnerability that could be thwarted by a harsh detention setting. Most facilities lack the resources and safe environments needed to pave the way for long-term recovery. Some jails and prisons have also been denying opioid users the medication for addiction treatment, as reported in a 2021 ACLU report. Though courts recently said that this denial likely violates the Eighth Amendment, and a contingent of jails and prisons started providing the MAT

(Medication Assisted Treatment) program, many don't offer adequate treatment.

Broderick experienced and witnessed mistreatment: the guards watched her defecate and shower, and she remembered them tormenting her, saying she was gaining weight. There was reportedly a serial rapist at Rosie's, to whom Broderick said the correction officers turned a blind eye. When it opened in 1988, Rosie's had once been considered state-of-the-art, costing $100 million to build, offering programs in food, gardening, and job training. Since then, however, it had "devolved into a torture chamber, where women are routinely abused, housed in unsanitary conditions, and denied medical and mental health services," wrote the granddaughter of Rose Singer, the reformer for whom this jail was named. "They are treated as less than human, not as our grandmothers, mothers, daughters and sisters."

After a month of white-knuckling sobriety, Broderick had little to do in jail. She was dealing with insomnia—the nights at Rosie's loud and bright—and she found the days endless. (Many incarcerated people told me they were either terrified or completely bored.) At most, she could read the books her dad had mailed her. Broderick lived on the second floor of Rosie's, in a specialized dorm for women dealing with mental health issues. That section could house up to 50 women, but it had only 15 when she was there. After a few months, Broderick got to know those other women. She learned of the opportunity to glean respect from the other women. "Women's prisons are more about creating family units," she explained. "As long as you weren't a total, absolute bitch—don't get into fights, cheat at cards, or hook up with someone's girlfriend, you know, you're civil—you're fine." She became an Inmate Counsel Representative, serving as a liaison between the women and the jail staff. That experience gave her keen insights into America's criminal justice system.

Most women at Rosie's, Broderick believed, shouldn't have been in there at all. "Addicts were common. That is generally the makeup of people coming in and going out. Or mentally ill. Women don't usually commit violent crimes. From what I've experienced inside, most people in there don't deserve to be there. There are other remedies and treatments that they're just not getting," she said. Only people who truly present a danger to society, like violent serial offenders, have reason to be locked up, she continued. Everyone else is in great need of resources, such as in-patient care, drug addiction counseling, or anger management. Incarceration, for most, is a waste of life.

She felt it was crucial that the nation shift its punitive drug laws, and she cited Portugal as a leader in drug policy that the United States could mirror. This European country had been a major drug capital in the 1980s, with high rates of crime, addiction, HIV, and mortality. Instead of criminalizing drug possession and consumption, in 2001 Portugal categorized it as a public health issue. Since then, drug users have been offered resources such as social workers, doctors, and attorneys; they discuss the availability of local services, treatments, and support networks (in some cases, drug users also may receive a warning or a small fine). This change in approach required—and resulted in—an enormous culture shift in the way Portuguese citizens viewed drugs and drug addiction. People were no longer called *drogados* ("junkies") but, rather, "people who use drugs" or "people with addiction disorders." It may seem like semantics, but these were meaningful distinctions, in that they emphasized the disorder instead of labeling those that suffered from it. The United States, Broderick argued, needed to follow suit, shifting its focus to the *reasons* a person is incarcerated, rather than the simple fact that they are.

While at Rikers, Broderick saw no support for women trying to break free of the incarceration cycle; Rosie's had even less supportive programming than did Rikers' men's jails. All that Broderick could find was religious programming, an acting class, a food prep course, and the Rikers Debate Project, which she joined. It seemed unfathomable to her that the city would be willing to spend billions of dollars to build new jails instead of investing the money in alternatives and public programs which, she believed, could effectively keep many people out of jails. While the city had allocated certain funds for these initiatives, it was nowhere near the price tag of $8.3 billion for its jails program.

The day Broderick was released, the correction officers woke her up at 5:00 a.m. and took her down to the intake area, where she waited until late afternoon to be processed. On her way out, she was handed a trash bag with her dead cellphone and her street clothes, which had been confiscated when she arrived. (The women COs, she recalled, laughed at her, saying, "You won't fit into these clothes; you got fat here!") She boarded the Q100 bus with her single-ride MetroCard from the Department of Correction, and was dropped off at a random stop in Queens. At last, she was free. However, she was now branded a felon.

Broderick couldn't secure an apartment lease and found it difficult to land a job. She finally located criminal-justice nonprofits in the city that offered opportunities for formerly incarcerated people. Though Broderick managed to stay clean, earn a bachelor's degree in criminology, and is now pursuing a graduate degree, she can't shake her felon status. She managed to break the cycle, but the criminal label follows her.

———

While Broderick was forced to serve her sentence, Tysheim Jenkins waited in Rikers for two years because he couldn't afford bail. In most of the world, bail for profit is not legal. In the United States, it's not only legal; it's a booming industry. The concept of bail is rooted in English common law, whereby defendants gave up land or valuables if they didn't show up for court dates. America took cash bail to a new level.

"America's open frontier and entrepreneurial spirit injected an innovation into the process: by the early 1800s, private businesses were allowed to post bail in exchange for payments from the defendants and the promise that they would hunt down the defendants and return them if they failed to appear. Commercial bail bond companies dominate the pre-trial release systems of only two nations, the United States and the Philippines," Adam Liptak wrote for the *New York Times*. Those who turn to the bail-bond industry pay high, nonrefundable premiums for their loans, even if they are found not guilty. In New York, a person pays the bail-bond agent between 6 and 10 percent of the stated bail amount as a deposit. If the defendant doesn't show up for the court date, the bail-bond agent takes the collateral to recoup the cost. But if the defendant appears for the court date, if they are found not guilty or are set free, they still won't get their money back.

Critics of the bail-bond industry see it as a corrupt cash grab. Some states have attempted to eliminate the cash-bail system. For instance, Kentucky, California, and Ohio have implemented various bail-reform initiatives; Republican Governor Chris Christie of New Jersey, who was a former federal prosecutor, championed bail reform and in 2014 signed legislation that eliminated mandatory cash bail, saying that it discriminated against people with little means. On April 1, 2019, New York joined suit, passing restrictions on cash bail and pretrial detention for nonviolent charges and misdemeanors. Though New York City implemented its bail-reform effort on January 1, 2020, it was met with fervent backlash and sensationalistic media headlines. Some accused advocates of this new legislation as causing an uptick in violent crime. Just a few months later, revisions were made, leaving it up to judges to set bail at their own discretion.

Tysheim Jenkins is someone who was greatly affected by the cash-bail system. In 2017, Jenkins, a Black man from the Bronx, was arrested on a drug charge. The judge set his bail at $3 million, an amount so astronomically high that Jenkins and his young family knew he'd have to sit in jail to wait for his court date. The bail amount dictated not only his path to Rikers but also his life there. He was barred from participating in jail programs. Housed with a high population of gang members, Jenkins said this was the worst part of his jail time: 40 of the 60 men he lived with were gang affiliated. He slept in a cell crawling with rats and roaches, on a mattress akin to a yoga mat unrolled across a metal frame. He ate horrible food, including food that had been thrown in the trash. After one mistrial, Jenkins again went to court, where he was found not guilty and was released.

"I had to fight for my life, with my mind, you know? It ended up working out in my favor, but that shit took a toll on me," he told me, his young daughters playing in the background. During his two years at Rikers, his baby was born. His two-year-old still didn't know who he was.

Children are collateral damage of the justice system, innocent bystanders forced to suffer without their parent. In the United States, one in every 28 children has a parent in lockup. While each situation is unique, many times the children face emotional, physical, and educational trauma, as well as financial instability. With only one parent able to work, it can be impossible to keep up with all the bills, now living in a broken home. This makes it easier to fall into poverty. The children can be stigmatized by fellow children and parents for having an incarcerated parent, becoming "that kid." Some become hopeless. Some become homeless. Many are forced to focus on survival rather than catching the school bus. These are the children of the desert, the city sidewalks, the town shelters, and the cross-country trains; they are the children who often don't have enough food to eat. The only thing remaining unbroken is the cycle.

Jenkins advocated for families and individuals of color caught in this system. When New York scaled back its bail-reform legislation in 2020, he wrote an op-ed that appeared in the Albany *Times Union*. "I don't want anyone to have to experience what I went through," Jenkins wrote. "But now that bail reform has been rolled back, black and brown New Yorkers like me will suffer the same fate. Judges will now have the ability to lock up even more marginalized people pretrial. Research has shown that increasing judges' authority will lead to the same outcome I was forced to endure, all because of a judge's perception."

When I asked Jenkins what he thought about the city's reform effort to build new, modern jails in the boroughs, like Moose he didn't believe it would change the nature of the system. "I don't think design can affect behavior. It's the people, not the design, that needs to change," Jenkins said. To those in power, incarcerated people—tried or not—were criminals. "It doesn't matter where the city puts the jails. What goes on inside the building isn't going to change. It will still be the same type of people running it, and it's systemically racist. It's the old, racist system of abuse that needs to change."

FIVE

Law Enforcement

A*merica's justice system is a* vast infrastructure of local, state, and national law enforcement officers, ranging from the police to correction officers to district attorney investigators to the Federal Bureau of Investigation (FBI). For most who get caught in the system, it's an encounter with the police that is the entry point.

Though the Department of Justice defines law enforcement as "the agencies and employees responsible for enforcing laws, maintaining public order, and managing public safety," some, whose experiences with law enforcement have been oppressive or violent, disagree. New York Police Department's police commissioner Dermot Shea recognized this in 2021 when he said, "Whether it was arresting runaway slaves, or enforcing unjust Jim Crow laws, it's been a stain on law enforcement's rich history. That is stained nevertheless. We have to acknowledge this truth. . . . These many years of racist policies and practices have caused—and, more importantly, continue to cause—immeasurable harm."

Some experts trace American policing back to the 1700s,

when "slave patrols" supported the system of slavery in the southern colonies. During this time, there was no formal police institution; instead, informal night watches, self-appointed groups, and local town sheriffs patrolled and controlled. "Southern cities like New Orleans, Savannah, and Charleston had paid full-time police who wore uniforms, were accountable to local civilian officials, and were connected to a broader criminal justice system. . . . They had the power to ride onto private property to ensure that slaves were not harboring weapons or fugitives, conducting meetings, or learning to read or write," wrote sociologist Alex S. Vitale in *The End of Policing*. When slavery was abolished, roughly 4 million African Americans were freed, but faced other forces: the white militia-style groups that replaced slave patrols. "They relentlessly and systematically enforced Black Codes, strict local and state laws that regulated and restricted access to labor, wages, voting rights, and general freedoms for formerly enslaved people," the NAACP said in its article, "The Origins of Modern Day Policing." Later, Black Codes were replaced with Jim Crow laws, which legally enforced segregation.

Other experts say America's first formal police force launched in 1838 in Boston, which was facing enormous waves of immigration, riots, and civil unrest. Boston Mayor Samuel Eliot launched the police force, modeled after the London Metropolitan Police, whose mission, according to sociologist Vitale, was to manage public disorder and protect the rich. Boston's formalized police force launched with 250 full-time officers paid with public dollars.

Just two hundred miles south, New York City, too, was experiencing a population boom, with immigrants—mainly Irish and German—arriving en masse. The city was becoming the country's epicenter of banking, media, transportation, and manufacturing, but violence, racism, and poverty were also pervasive. New York, like Boston, modeled its new police department on the London Metropolitan Police, and in 1845, the New York Police Department officially launched with its newly printed rules and regulations. This was a time of great corruption, particularly as the political organization of Tammany Hall gained tremendous power, working with the police to gain more control. It wasn't just the NYPD facing corruption, though. "The late 19th century was the era of political machines, so police captains and sergeants for each precinct were often picked by the local political party ward leader, who often owned taverns or ran street gangs that intimidated voters," writes Olivia Waxman in *Time* magazine. "They then were able to use police to harass opponents of that particular political party, or provide payoffs for officers to turn a blind eye to allow illegal drinking, gambling and prostitution."

As the nation grew, so did its police. By the 1880s, all major American cities had established their own official police departments. Today, the NYPD exists as the largest municipal police force in the nation.

———

Throughout history, there have been myriad definitions of criminal behavior and various ways to deal with it. When certain methods are deemed ineffective, inhumane, or irrelevant, attempts at reform are made.

One particular instance of police reform happened in New

York City in the 1980s, in the wake of fiscal crisis, panic, and paranoia. The prior decade was defined by violence and up-heaval: the nation's largest city, cheerily known as the Big Apple, earned a new nickname, Fear City. As tourists entered the city, police union members handed out welcome pamphlets: "Welcome to Fear City: A Survival Guide for Visitors to the City of New York," with a hooded skeleton of Death pictured on the cover. "Until things change, stay away from New York City, if you possibly can." In July of 1977, a blackout struck most of New York City, while the serial killer calling himself "Son of Sam" had been murdering young brunette women in cold blood. At the same time, fires erupted across the South Bronx, displacing 250,000 residents. Calls came from all corners of the city de-manding more public safety services, but resources were severely limited by the fiscal crisis. By the end of the decade, the NYPD had lost 9,000 sworn personnel; the overpopulated jails were se-verely understaffed.

By the early 1970s, the emergency phone number 911 was gaining traction. By the 1980s, the police were receiving millions of emergency calls each year, demanding much of their resources. A shift occurred. "Policing changed from a preventative mode into a reactive mode," former Police Commissioner Bill Bratton wrote in a 2008 article for the Project for Public Spaces. "We took our police officers off their beats and lost the intimate con-tact and partnerships that those beat officers had for many years with neighborhoods. And our investigation of crime was always after the fact. American police became reactive, and lost control, and, in effect, depoliced our streets."

Stepping in to help, the Vera Institute of Justice studied

the NYPD's tactics and operations and discovered a profound disconnect between cops and communities. The nonprofit organization worked with the NYPD to launch a pilot program that aimed to create better bonds between cops and communities, while also promoting public safety. The program was rooted in community policing, a philosophy that invests in prevention rather than reaction. This practice puts a beat cop on a regular route, where he is supposed to establish relationships with the locals, understand their needs, anticipate conflict, and develop solutions working with the community. In the summer of 1984, the Community Patrol Officer pilot program kicked off in Brooklyn's 72nd precinct. An assortment of cops were tapped for the program, ranging from rookies to veterans to community-minded cops to the "go-lock-'em-up" guys. They were now Community Patrol Officers (CPOs), responsible for a stretch of blocks, facilitating "long-range peace keeping and crime control objectives in the beat area." The CPOs distributed fliers that featured a cartoon image of a CPO with a child on either side of him. The flyer proclaimed the CPO has a "sincere interest in helping the people improve living conditions in the neighborhood."

Among the CPOs was rookie cop Pat Russo, the grandson of Italian immigrants and the son of a Brooklyn businessman. Russo entered the department just a year before and had joined the NYPD boxing team. After winning a boxing championship at Madison Square Garden against the New York Fire Department, Russo earned respect from his peers, despite his rookie status. While Russo believed it was possible for cops to do good work, he'd also witnessed hypocrisy and apathy in the ranks.

"The precinct commanders weren't accountable to the crime in the area," Russo recalled. "They said, 'Just don't have corruption and give out tickets to generate revenue for the city.' That's all they really cared about. They didn't care about crime spikes in their areas." Russo felt inspired to help change this.

Assigned to Brooklyn's Sunset Park, a lower-income, mostly Hispanic community, the young CPO Russo learned people's names, got to know local groups, and heard their concerns. "I was like Andy Griffith. I had a small ten-block area and I was in charge," Russo told me. The most pressing issue, he learned, was the gangs and drug dealers hanging out on a specific block—in police speak, a "hot spot." A hot spot can be as distinct as a single block or intersection where crime routinely occurs, often between feuding groups.

Hearing the locals' concerns, Russo reacted fast. Arrests were the force's typical reaction to criminal behavior; this is how they were trained. Within the first month, Russo and his team, along with the Bureau of Narcotic Enforcement, made 100 arrests. To Russo's shock, the community was outraged. A community member explained to him that the arrests were creating a cycle of violence and poverty: the arrests gave teenagers felony records, making it nearly impossible for them to get higher education, jobs, or leases, which then created more setbacks and obstacles, and gave them few options beyond criminal activity or joining gangs. Also, the community member added, these teenagers were replaceable. Even if the police continued to arrest the kids, the crime leader in Sunset Park could easily find other kids to do his work.

Hot spots tend to be in settings of concentrated poverty, but by another measure, they can be some of the more costly neighborhoods in the city. The area can have so many arrests that taxpayers end up spending over a million dollars a year to incarcerate multiple people from these places. This phenomenon, termed "million dollars blocks," was discovered after Columbia University's Center for Spatial Research and its Justice Mapping Center used maps and rarely accessible information from police departments to find these high-arrest spots. The dollars, they argue, could be better invested in these areas to help prevent crime, violence, and incarceration in the first place.

Russo regrouped. He saw the importance of going for the root of the problem rather than simply scratching the surface with multiple arrests of young people. "We gave them all felon arrest records because they were doing street sales hand-to-hand. It was a major setback in their lives," Russo said. Working with the Brooklyn District Attorney's Office and the Bureau of Narcotic Enforcement, they arrested the leader of the crime network (who was guilty of several murders), who was sentenced to prison. Without the crime leader running the block, the community had its street back; the hot spot cooled. Russo began looking at ways to keep the kids occupied, so they wouldn't get caught up in gangs or hand-to-hand deals.

Meanwhile, it seemed the community policing pilot program was meeting with some success. Most locals said they felt more comfortable with their CPOs than with a regular police officer, according to a Vera report. By 1989, the community policing program had expanded to all 75 precincts. By 1991, every precinct had 10 CPO officers. Ultimately, the community policing philosophy didn't become New York City's—or any other

American city's—dominant style of policing. According to the New York City consulting firm Public Works Partners, three main barriers stood in the way of that happening, including a "lack of consistent political will, standardization, and evaluation measures." Instead, a more punitive approach triumphed.

Other policing tactics gained steam. In 1990, the NYPD implemented "zero tolerance" for petty crimes, a policy based on the "Broken Windows" theory. First described in a 1982 *Atlantic Monthly* article by George Kelling and James Wilson, this theory promoted the idea that cracking down on smaller issues and minor crimes in neighborhoods would prevent major crimes from happening. "We tend to overlook another source of fear— the fear of being bothered by disorderly people. Not violent people, nor, necessarily, criminals, but disreputable or obstreperous or unpredictable people: panhandlers, drunks, addicts, rowdy teenagers, prostitutes, loiterers, the mentally disturbed," the authors wrote. By addressing neighborhood disorder, citizens would feel safer and businesses and communities could thrive, they argued. Kelling later wrote in a *Politico* article that "good" Broken Windows policing encourages cops to work with local partners, such as social workers, teachers, and medical personnel. The Broken Windows theory, however, was widely misinterpreted, he said. Minor crime arrests were supposed to be a last resort. Instead, they became the first.

Police forces across the nation adopted the Broken Windows theory and made mass arrests for offenses like painting graffiti, selling untaxed cigarettes, and squeegeeing car windows for cash. Incarcerated populations ballooned. Critics of Broken Windows accused police of targeting people of color, flooding the justice system with low-level offenders, and further fracturing relationships between the police and communities of color. The methods to enforce Broken Windows included stop-and-frisk, a highly controversial police practice.

The stop-and-frisk policy began under Mayor Rudy Giuliani and Police Commissioner Bill Bratton. As Bratton wrote in his book *Turnaround*, "Mayor Giuliani was a former federal prosecutor. He liked putting criminals in jail." Called "Terry stop" nationwide, the stop-and-frisk program allowed the cops to stop anyone suspected of committing a crime and search them for weapons. The practice then gained serious traction in New York City during the Bloomberg administration. Over the 20 years this policy was in effect, the NYPD conducted millions of stop-and-frisks, many with racist underpinnings: under this policy between 2004 and 2012, more than 80 percent of people stopped by the NYPD were Black and Latino people. Stop-and-frisks sometimes lead to violence, even death. "Stop-and-frisk became a central issue in the 2013 city mayoral race because of a concern that the program unconstitutionally targeted communities of color. The program's supporters disputed this, insisting that stop-and-frisk was essential for fighting crime in such a huge city," the Brennan Center reported. But there was no evidence that ramping up this tactic made communities safer. Support for the policy diminished and stop-and-frisk incidents declined. "Given this large-scale effort, one might expect crime generally, and murder specifically, to increase as stops tapered off between 2012 and 2014. Instead . . . the murder rate fell while the number of stops declined. In fact, the biggest fall occurred precisely when the number of stops also fell by a large amount—in 2013," the Brennan Center reported. In 2013, a federal judge found NYPD's use of stop-and-frisk to be unconstitutional against people of color. Then, tragedy happened.

In 2014, Eric Garner, a Black man suspected of selling loosies* in Staten Island, was killed by police. Police accused Garner of selling untaxed cigarettes; he denied it and resisted, but the cops threw Garner to the ground in a choke hold, holding him until he died. A video of the incident went viral, igniting outrage. It was emblematic of how unarmed Black people in America were being killed at the hands of white police officers, continuing a trend that had been growing since the beginning of policing in America. National demands mounted to "defund the police."

Today, with over 18,000 local police departments nationwide, police face multiple accusations of exercising force and of abusing their power, despite fevered demands for reform and defunding. Similar to the operation of local jails, police forces have their own training programs, policies, protocols, and practices; there is little uniform structure or policy governing the standards of the police forces. Any attempt to address American policing standards is an extremely divisive and controversial topic. Within these arguments, there are often just two choices: Defund the Police or Fund the Police, Fuck the Police or Blue Lives Matter. Perhaps there are answers outside of these binary viewpoints.

A coterie of cops and correction officers in New York City believe they have an answer. With firsthand knowledge of the

---

* Single cigarettes.

system, these law enforcement officials are going outside the justice system to prevent crime, instead of policing it.

——

After rookie cop Pat Russo cleared the hot spot in Sunset Park, a neighbor told him the local kids needed something to do with their idle hands or they'd fall prey to gangs, violence, or illicit activity. There were few programs to keep them occupied. Drawing from his own passion, Russo was a dedicated boxer who believed in the sport's power to discipline, encourage, and instill dedication. In 1986, Russo opened Brooklyn's only free boxing gym for kids.

The Cops & Kids Boxing Gym offered kids and teenagers an outlet in the ring, removing them from boredom or toxic environments while creating bonds with law enforcement officials who were also boxers (though it wasn't an intended consequence, Russo said the program could also serve as a recruiting tool for the department). "It attracted the kid that wants to be part of something that's perceived as tough," Russo said. "Instead of wearing Latin Kings colors and all that stuff, they're wearing Cops & Kids jackets, walking in Brownsville and Flatbush, and the toughest areas of the city."

Kids came from across the boroughs to train, many discovering a profound love of boxing and a healthy way to channel their energy and develop their focus. Among them was a young boy named Joel, who'd come to the program because he liked the idea of fighting cops in the ring. He didn't hate cops, but he definitely didn't see them as nice guys with good advice or help with homework. After joining the Cops & Kids program, his image of law enforcement changed: he saw the police as mentors and motivators, people he could trust and look to for guidance and inspiration. The boxing gym also brought together kids from different backgrounds and ethnicities—kids Joel might never have met or befriended otherwise, now bonded by their love of boxing.

Russo saw how this free boxing program was transforming kids and giving them a safe, inspiring space. Invested in the power of the program, Russo teamed up with Rikers Island correction officer Gary Stark. In 1990, they opened another Cops & Kids program, this time in the projects of Staten Island.* At the time, Park Hill in Staten Island was one of New York City's deadliest housing projects, an area consumed with gang violence and haunted by the crack epidemic, earning it the name "Crack Hill." Members of the legendary hip-hop group Wu-Tang Clan grew up there, where one member recalled, "It was a nightmare, you know, but it was home."

Since the Cops & Kids program launched in Park Hill—and other programs, like the African Refuge Center, moved into the neighborhood—violence seemed to subside. Generally speaking, New York City in the 1990s seemed to be improving from the days when the NYPD and the Vera Institute launched their pilot community policing program. By 2017, New York City had the lowest incarceration rate of all large U.S. cities, with the lowest

---

* The program went on to train pro boxers and future Olympians, including Bruce Carrington for Team USA, Richardson Hitchins for Haiti, Christina Cruz for Team USA, and Marcus Browne, who competed in the 2012 Summer Olympics.

incidence of crime. When the pandemic hit, in 2020, however, things took a turn for the worse.

Like many parts of the country, Park Hill experienced a spike in murders. Gang wars among the Paybacc Crips, Only the Africans, and the Young Paper Chasers were at a new high, and innocent people were paying the price. In November 2020, a 52-year-old woman was shot in the head in the lobby of a Park Hill apartment building. A young Golden Gloves boxer, Grashino Yancy, was shot and killed at a Park Hill barbecue. Just up the street, another man was shot twice that same day. Russo knew it was crucial to reopen the boxing gym as soon as possible. When the city gave notice that gyms could reopen, Cops & Kids did so immediately.

To understand why the Cops & Kids mentors, the NYPD Boxing Team, and the local children and teens were so invested in this program, I paid a visit to Park Hill. The boxing gym lives in one of the monolithic brick buildings of this Section 8 housing development. Many housing developments for which Section 8 vouchers can be used were designed and built in the mid-twentieth century, when the hopes were to progress from the squalid tenements of the nineteenth century. However, the realities of Section 8 housing can be far from ideal. Park Hill residents have held protests and have reported to the media the squalid conditions and their landlord's negligence. Every one to three years, the U.S. Department of Housing and Urban Development sends a representative to perform inspections. Still, dangerous mold grows in the hallways and apartment units, and the buildings battle roach and rodent infestations and deal with broken elevators, blood-splattered walls, and long stretches of freezing nights without heat.

I entered the lobby of one of the identical brick buildings where the gym resides. The lobby, with its cement-block walls, yellowed linoleum floors, and flickering fluorescent lights, was buzzing with activity. Residents shuffled in and out of apartment units; others hung out in the communal space, rolling cigarettes or trading gossip. I made my way through the lobby and entered the door to the gym.

Inside, the smell of steel, baby powder, and sweat laced the air. A bright yellow room welcomed me with the words *Park Hill Boxing Club* painted across one wall. Photos of children, teenagers, and pro boxers who have gone through the program lined the other walls, along with framed newspaper articles and posters of legendary fights. A hand-painted mural of two pro boxers stood proud. One lone pugilist practiced his uppercuts in the ring.

The kids would be arriving soon, along with Coach Gary Stark, now retired from corrections. Pat Russo had arrived early and told me it was a good day to be dropping by: today was the tournament between Park Hill and Berry Houses, another housing project on Staten Island.

"Yo, Joel!" Russo called out to the man in the ring.

The pugilist looked up and smiled. "What's up, Patty?" He ducked out of the ring so Russo could introduce us. This was the same boy, Joel, who had boxed at the Cops & Kids program in Sunset Park. Since then, the young boy had grown up, joined the Air Force, and become a police officer—a path for which he credits his boxing mentors. Based on his own experience, Joel understood the direct impact the boxing program had on his life, and he believes it is of the utmost importance to help out at Cops & Kids. He barely has time to sleep, but he feels strongly about helping kids and the community.

It can be difficult to get law enforcement on the record, but Joel was ready to talk. "Policing is punishment. That's how it's set up," Joel told me. "I never hated cops, but you're not going to look at cops as people you want to see on an everyday basis. . . . If you want to take away that negative idea of them, reroute that, you have to have more community-based programs that police do."

Many situations he has encountered as a police officer Joel didn't feel trained for. A social worker would have been a better mediator than a police officer, he believed. Most cops seldom face violent scenarios: much of their time is spent writing detailed reports, being conflict mediators and quasi–social workers. "We prepare police officers for a job we imagine them to have rather than the role they actually perform," Roge Karma wrote in a *Vox* article. "We train police to be warriors—and then send them out to be social workers." "Police are hired disproportionately from the military, trained in military-style academies that focus largely on the deployment of force and law, and equipped with lethal weapons at all times, and they operate within a culture that takes pride in warriorship, combat, and violence."

Like other graduates of the boxing program, Joel wholeheartedly believes that free programs—not just run by cops, but also by members of the community—function as crime prevention. "Boxing naturally attracts the tough kids," Joel said, pointing to photos on the wall. "These are troubled kids, and boxing gives you a positive way of getting out your energy. When you actually become really good at something, you're confident. You can de-escalate things easier. If I know how to fight or box, I'm less likely to get into fights outside. You don't threaten or challenge people; you don't feel like there's something to prove. You're a boxer. You come to the gym to compete. It's a different mentality." While boxing is about self-transformation, it also builds bridges among different groups that might not otherwise be friends. "You look at all the kids, it's the United Nations. . . . Everyone is so diverse and comes under the one culture of boxing. . . . It's what makes boxing special," Joel said.

Young pugilists began flooding into the gym. Hip-hop pounded through the speakers, the energy up. As if sensing Coach Stark was about to arrive, the beat dropped and the door swung open. Pushing 5 foot 9 inches and thick with muscle, Coach Gary Stark entered wearing a baseball hat, a gold chain, his ears pierced with gold studs. He had swag, maybe even a slight limp, as he crossed the room. The kids brightened as Coach said his hellos, patting kids on the head. Clearly everyone here adored Stark. He helped the kids learn how to drive, get their driver's licenses, and made sure they didn't skip school. NYPD Boxing pays Stark $900 a month, but Russo said Coach spends more of his own scratch to help provide kids with things they need. The 61-year-old coach walked with gravitas, like this retired CO had seen some shit.

Raised in Flatbush, Brooklyn, by a single mother from Guatemala (his dad left when Stark was seven years old), Stark's family was on welfare and often didn't have enough food to eat. Stark started boxing at 17, which instilled in him discipline, ethics, and razor-sharp awareness. After spending his teen years boxing, Stark went into corrections at age 24. The decision, he explained, was more practical than emotional: his best friend's sister's boyfriend was a correction officer and made $19,000 a year—in those days, that was a nice chunk of change that would help support his young son. However, he'd have to stop boxing; at the time, he was training for the Golden Gloves, but he was told it was a liability because he could be injured while boxing and not able to come to work. During the Giuliani administration, Stark was assigned to Rikers Island, where he saw record numbers of people locked up. He watched cops arrest people for issues with drug addiction, homelessness, and mental illness, and the system put them behind bars. No one, it seemed, was addressing the root causes of these issues. Working on Rikers was draining and emotionally exhausting for Stark. "It turns your stomach sometimes, the way the system is," Stark said. "There were kids in there that shouldn't be there. . . . [Giuliani] said, 'Let's lock them up!' That's not what you do. They should have programs for everyone who needs these programs. . . . But *where* are the programs?" Focusing on prevention programs "puts good people in charge," Stark said, looking at his students. "My goal with the boxing: taking kids off the street, introducing them to boxing and see how far we can go."

I brought up New York City's multibillion-dollar program to build new jails. Joel voiced his opinion. "I understand the challenges some might have with Rikers. They say to fix it, or close it and build new jails. But the fact of the matter is, do you want to deal with the problem when it gets there? Or do you want to prevent it from happening? It's like fixing something when it's broke versus"—he paused—"not letting it break." It was crime prevention, not reaction, that was changing lives and keeping communities safer. As long as there was a free, cool place for kids to go, the kids would be there. The nation needs more programs, Joel said, not new jails.

Larry, another cop who'd dropped into the gym to train, chimed in. "Programs in the community are *way* better than building new jails! No matter what hood you're from, what gang you're a part of . . . everyone plays together. . . . The results we have here are kids become entrepreneurs, firefighters, they join the military, they're aspiring to be lawyers. . . . You have a program that costs pennies compared to what's going into incarcerating people." He was right. Incarcerating one person in a New York City jail costs over half a million dollars per year while, for instance, the Park Hill boxing gym costs $50,000 to $60,000 per year to run.

The gym is funded by boxing championship fundraisers and private donations. To receive government funding, applicants often need to show results in concrete numbers. Free programs, like Cops & Kids, can have trouble getting public funding, as it's difficult to measure the success of the programs, and such documentation demands time, money, and long-term tracking. Pat Russo said they don't have the resources to follow gym participants for years, to show how the program affects their lives in the long run. Without these stats, programs can lose funding, support, and ultimately close, as was the case with the Sunset Park boxing gym. In 2007, the boxing ring was removed from the city-owned recreation center when the Parks and Recreation department decided to repurpose the space for other after-school programs. Many people rallied to save the gym, including New York Senator Chuck Schumer, all to no avail. The gym was closed.

Larry said that if the city shuts down programs, it sends a message to communities. When the city prioritizes new jails over programs and resources, it speaks volumes to children. "They're threatening with these new jail buildings: 'This is going to happen to you.' So now what the kids goin' to think? 'You building it because you think I'm a troublemaker. What I'm gonna be? Ima be a troublemaker.' But if you build programs like these, it don't matter where you're from, what hood, what gang. It's boxing."

Though the guys at Cops & Kids believed wholeheartedly that crime prevention exists in free programs, they are not in the majority among their peers. A 2017 study conducted by Pew Research found that 56 percent of cops agree that aggressive tactics are more effective than a courteous approach in "certain areas of the city." Fifty-six percent of the cops said they became more "callous toward people since they started their job." The American tradition of aggressive policing had persisted, despite some cops investing their time outside the system. The sixth cause of death for men of any ethnicity ages 25 to 29 is to be killed by the police.

As the boxing tournament was about to begin, spectators pressed in around the ring. Everyone was engaged. I overheard one parent call out playfully to a kid, "Hey, why you smiling?"

The child beamed. "Because life's too beautiful not to."

I smiled, too. Everyone—cops, kids, parents, volunteers, spectators—seemed close, respectful, playful, and above all dedicated to the art of boxing. The enthusiasm was infectious. Turning to the cops, I asked if there were others in law enforcement who felt the same way as they did about investing in more programs.

"I can't speak for every cop. But I know that ones like him," Larry said, nodding to Joel, "like me, know that we need more programs like this. You can't build jails and then think that these kids won't fill them."

Joel shook his head. "If you build it, they will come."

SIX

An "Award-Winning" Jail

nlike the cop volunteers in Park Hill, New York City officials—like John Haviland, Jeremy Bentham, and the Quakers—believed in the power of new design to transform the system. To be best in class, the Borough-Based Jails were required to use the direct-supervision model, considered by most in the field as the most humane of correctional design.

I'd heard praise of this model from the justice architect Greg Cook, who was proud of his direct-supervision design in Hot Springs, Arkansas. Since the jail had opened in 2015, the jail had won multiple awards, both for its architecture and its management style. By certain standards, this jail is considered exemplary, which I felt made it worth investigating.

Lieutenant Donald Ansley at the Garland County Sheriff's Office responded almost immediately, saying they'd be delighted to give me a tour. This standing invite was a departure from the red tape I typically faced when working with jails and prison staff. In my experience, it usually required weeks or months of background checks, media credentials, advanced scheduling, and security clearance—that is, if they allowed me in at all. It was another reminder that each jail in America has its own identity, protocol, rules, and authority.

Before the sun crowned on the horizon, I took off from Newark Liberty International Airport in the dead heat of July. It was even swampier when I landed in Arkansas.

———

Hot Springs, known for its natural thermal waters and historic row of bathhouses, is where notorious gangsters like Al Capone, "Machine Gun" Kelly, and "Pretty Boy" Floyd used to unwind during Prohibition. The eclectic Victorian bathhouses still stand, but in the 1920s, brothels, speakeasies, and gambling dens operated across from bathhouse row. Gambling was a huge source of income for the town, and according to the local history museum, the local police often turned a blind eye. Today, Hot Springs remains a hotbed of illicit activity. While the main drag still hosts tourists seeking a soak, the town has one of the nation's highest crime rates. Close to Interstate 40, a major drug pipeline, Hot Springs residents struggle with meth and fentanyl abuse. Strict drug laws were implemented to slash drug sales and use. For those who get busted and are sent to jail, they're locked up in the new direct-supervision facility.

The Garland County Detention Center rests on the edge of town, a few miles from the Arkansas Alligator Farm and Petting Zoo and the food distribution center for the Cherokee Chief Indian Ministry. I drove past the Wash-N-Go, the American Legion Hall, the Tobacco Junction, a motorcycle repair shop, and the shuttered newsroom for the free local paper *The Thrifty Nickel*. Eying an unassuming sign for the jail, I pulled onto a winding drive, where a contemporary building with sloped roofs and a brick façade came into view.

Surrounded by mountains and resting on 57 lush acres, this setting was a far cry from Rikers Island's isolated trash heap surrounded by razor wire. Nothing indicated this was, in fact, a jail—not even perimeter fencing. It could be mistaken for a government headquarters or even a school. The American and Arkansas flags anchored a circular drive in the front lobby entrance. Out back was a garden, an award-winning greenhouse, and beehives for honey extraction.

When it opened, the Garland County Detention Center was one of the town's largest construction projects. Costing $42 million, the price tag was almost three times the county's total operating budget. The Garland County staff believes it was worth it. The incarceration experience should help change the incarcerated people's ways of thinking and provide them with the tools they need to be successful. Their ethos earned national attention and acclaim from the American Jail Association, the National Institute of Corrections, the American Correctional Association, *Law Enforcement Coordinating Committee News*, and *U.S. News and World Report*. In 2018 and in 2020, correction officers from Garland County won the Correctional Supervisor of the Year Award from the American Jail Association. The jail also earned the award of "Best Project over $6 Million," presented by the Arkansas chapter of the American Concrete Institute. Many of the staff at Garland County are Certified Jail Officers, a voluntary certification program that educates frontline officers on topics such as incarcerated people's rights, suicide prevention, stress management, hygiene and sanitation, and how to problem solve.

In 2021, the American Jail Association gave recognition to Garland County for having the most Certified Jail Officers in a single facility—64 in total.

As the receptionist logged my ID, I studied the lobby. Greg Cook chose brick and glass materials, which he said suggested a theme of openness and transparency. Art made by incarcerated people hung on one wall. On another wall, the original steel bars from the old jail gave a symbolic nod to How Far We've Come.

A door slammed and an Arkansan wearing a polo shirt, loose khakis, and boat shoes approached me. Lieutenant Donald Ansley had recently been put on the night shift, but he came in this morning to give me a tour. Ansley had been in corrections for 27 years, and he served on the so-called transition team when they moved from the old jail to Cook's direct-supervision design. Ansley was primed to discuss the differences between direct and indirect supervision. Joining us was Captain Belinda Cosgrove, a blond local with a warm smile, who'd also served on the transition team and was the first female captain in this operation. In 2018, she won the National Correctional Supervisor of the Year award.

"Shall we?" Ansley nodded to a metal detector and fortified entrance.

———

The door clanged, my muscles clenched, and a corridor the length of a football field stretched out before us. To those inside, this is "Main Street," a bright, sanitized hallway with the sterile whiff of bureaucracy. Fluorescent lights reflected off the polished linoleum floor; the walls stacked in concrete masonry.

Identical gray doors lined both sides: to my right, the doors led to the dorms, and to my left, the doors led to services. One of the dorm doors opened and a group of six men in matching jumpsuits chatted as they rounded onto Main Street. Clocking me, they stopped dead in their tracks.

"Teach?" one guy called out.

"No." I shook my head.

They talked among themselves, then ambled on.

"Lunch," Ansley explained. "If they get in a fight, something like that, or if they're really mentally ill, they'll need to be escorted. But the guys who come in here for murder, you'll see them walking around the hallways."

As at other jails, most incarcerated people here have not been tried. They wait at Garland County for their court dates, some having calls with their lawyers on video chat, others not meeting their lawyers until they're escorted into the courtroom. Garland County can hold up to 476 incarcerated people, and at this time there were 394. This ensured direct supervision's tenet of holding only up to 80 percent capacity, so staff has flexibility to classify incarcerated people and place them in corresponding living situations.

Donald Ansley led us into the intake and release area— what Greg Cook considered "the car engine" of the facility. This is where people are processed into and out of jail. Cook took care to put this area and the sally port—the secured entry point where incarcerated people are transferred to the jail—on the jail's backside so as to shield this process from public view. At many jails, this process can take days, a grueling experience that can haunt people long after they're out. At Garland County, intake resembled a doctor's waiting room, except for the four people who were waiting to be processed, the landlines stationed around the room, and the holding cells (to be used if anyone misbehaved). Intake is where the first introduction to direct supervision occurs, where newcomers learn this model's playbook: if they're cooperative and follow the rules, they'll receive more privileges; if they act out, they'll be locked in a cell. The direct-supervision model uses an objective classification system, whereby incarcerated people are assessed for danger levels, health issues, and additional needs, then they are assigned the appropriate custody level and programs. This was the first of many steps designed to transform the experience not only of the incarcerated people but also that of the correction officers.

In traditional jails, staff members were called "guards," often used brute force, isolated incarcerated people, and observed them through barriers. This method is still used in places like Rikers. The direct-supervision model, in contrast, requires officers to undergo a one-week National Institute of Corrections Direct Supervision course. Passing the Certified Jail Officer Test isn't mandatory, but will earn an officer a higher salary. The main requirement is experience. Knowing the incarcerated population is key. Each officer serves a post for two months and is expected to know each person by name, to anticipate their needs, and to sense when trouble is brewing, which theoretically earns the CO respect in return. While the Garland County staff believes this style is a vast improvement from the old way of running things, direct supervision was difficult—if not impossible—for some former employees at the old jail to accept. They estimated that only 15 percent of the original staff was able to make the transition to direct supervision. The rest left.

"A lot of them could not adapt," Garland County's security director, Captain Ron Halverson, told me.

"The days of hiring a huge football player, throwing someone into their cell, those days are gone," Captain Cosgrove chimed in. "We need people who have excellent communication skills, who want to be that mentor, the professional leader in the housing unit."

"You have to literally change the culture," Ansley added. "You can't resort . . . to the old ways. The old staff who weren't into it, they didn't make the cut."

Garland County went outside corrections to tap new staff—some even had no corrections experience. They also pulled people from the state's prison system. A young CO who'd left the Arkansas Department of Correction to come to Garland County said it was much better here. When I asked him how it had been working at the state penitentiary, he cringed.

"Horrible," he said. "I rode a horse. We worked them in the fields. . . . They picked corn. . . . I was wound up like a spring over there. This is way better. . . . Here, it's a lot more safe, and helps people not come back. Here, we care a lot more about people."

Transitioning to direct supervision didn't just affect the staff; it also affected incarcerated people. "They were used to running the unit," a CO said. "All of a sudden, a CO was present in the dorm at all times, creating a very different atmosphere."

"They've never known anything different, you know, from

the old-school way where inmates run the units," Captain Halverson said. "The CO will go get the key and go get a guy, and that guy will go beat everybody up and makes everyone or that gang do what they're supposed to do. But we do not permit inmates to have authority over other inmates. *We* have all the authority. *We* make all the decisions. That's why we have a deputy in the living unit."

I thought about Moose's insights that gangs could never be dismantled—that inside, the gang leaders ruled. It seemed the direct-supervision model might flip that hierarchy on its head. Here, the COs interacted with the incarcerated people and even played games with them. Their role was more akin to officers' roles in Norway, where staff members are trained to prepare incarcerated people for success once they are released.

Back on Main Street, Ansley asked if I wanted to see a dorm unit. "Yes, please," I said, and I followed the lieutenant through the secured doors.

Inside, the noise level was deafening. Seventy men in orange V-neck jumpsuits stood around in small groups, their voices barreling off the walls. Except in places like Eastern State Penitentiary where the acoustics were essential to make people feel more isolated, little attention was typically paid to the acoustics in detention settings, causing some incarcerated people to suffer nausea, headaches, and even hearing loss from the unrelenting sound. While this room was carpeted and used a selection of softer materials to absorb sound, the cacophony could still be unbearable.

"Female entering!" Ansley bellowed into the room.

The room fell silent, 140 eyes on me.

Noticing the sudden silence, the CO looked up from his desk, which displayed multiple computers with ongoing clerical work and live security footage of the dorm. ("There are no dark corners here," Ansley had said.) Strategically stationed in the center of the dorm, the CO could be reached at any time and also could see everyone clearly from his place.

"We're doing commissary, so they're getting their candy and bags of instant coffee," the CO said, walking over to us. "They get a little hyper." The men listened in and ate snacks, like I was the show.

The dorm had high ceilings, stretching up two stories. Both floors housed cells, which remained unlocked so the men could come and go as they pleased around the dorm. Some chose to hang out on couches in the communal living-room area, others could play basketball in the adjoining rec room, where the windows poured in sunlight and allowed a glimpse of Arkansas's wooded hills. (Daylight, Greg Cook told me, was the most important feature.)

The CO explained that this was his first job ever in a detention facility. He worked in the unit unarmed, save for his pepper spray. Outside, a rover and a supervisor were on standby with tasers in case things escalated beyond his management. In the early days of the job, the CO explained, he'd felt overwhelmed, outnumbered. After experiencing the inside and seeing how things worked, he adapted quickly. He knows each incarcerated person by name. Sometimes, he'll play basketball with them. This was all part of the direct-supervision approach, Ansley explained: the CO speaks to most or all of the incarcerated people at least once a day and makes eye contact when doing so.

"You want to see a cell?" the CO asked.

The three of us entered one of the ground-floor cells, while the remaining men lingered around in the living room. Here, cell doors didn't have bean holes,* since residents were allowed to eat outside their cells. A metal toilet stood in a corner, while a plastic stool (instead of the typical steel stool bolted to the ground) rested under a wooden desk, on top of which was a program pamphlet and books. The top and bottom bunks were neatly made; beside the bottom bunk was another book and a pair of reading glasses. Towels hung like curtains from the bunk, presumably for privacy, a right routinely stripped from most incarcerated people. A light switch allowed them to control the lighting, considered a luxury in many detention settings.

As we exited the dorm, the CO told me that the longest time someone was incarcerated waiting for trial here was four years.

———

We continued the tour. In another dorm unit, incarcerated men rested in dim lighting after working their morning shifts. Carpeting softened the linoleum floor and a library cart with books rested in a corner. In a small offshoot room, five guys in jumpsuits played poker.

As we continued down Main Street, Ansley pointed out the rooms for video court, doctor visits, and GED studying and testing. This jail, I learned, was one of the state's largest GED testing sites, run by National Park College Adult Education. If

---

* Slang for food ports.

someone earns their GED inside, they're eligible for a 50 percent cut in their college tuition in their first year. Garland offers 25 different trade programs, the Garland County Detention Center Learning Greenhouse, the Workforce Alliance for Growth in the Economy, anger-management classes, and a Love and Logic Parenting Class, supported by 200 community volunteers and a chaplain. Of all the programs available, the most popular and coveted is the substance-abuse program.

The 90-day substance-abuse program is run by counselor Marty Haynes, a recovered addict who has been incarcerated himself (this jail offers full-time work to formerly incarcerated people). Having someone like Haynes run the program implies he understands their situation. At first, Haynes admitted he was leery of working for the government. After interviewing, touring the space, and seeing the robust programs offered at Garland County, Haynes saw the potential. The people going through the substance-abuse programs, he said, are just like those he helps on the outside: "They're inmates to the county, but they're clients to me." His primary goal, he explained, is to give incarcerated people the tools to break the cycle of addiction and incarceration.

When I entered the women's substance abuse unit, twenty women in navy jumpsuits curved over tables covered with Bibles and lunch trays, eating their crackers and peanut butter sandwiches. Each morning, the women rise at 7:30 and head to both group therapy and one-on-one counseling. Everyone eats lunch together. Afternoons are for individual programming and classes.

"There aren't really other county jails that offer a substance-abuse program like this," said a 42-year-old blond woman with a tiny star tattooed under one eye. "It's really rehabilitating here, not punishing. . . . I didn't want to accept that I had a disease. Mr. Marty has a way of getting us to accept that fact, and he gives us the tools to deal with our addictions. They let us know we're not crazy, we're not thugs, or bad people. We just made bad choices."

A 34-year-old woman chimed in. Since she was 13 years old, she had been struggling with addiction. "I've realized that doing it on the inside and transitioning to a program on the outside is really the only way I feel successful doing it. Because I always miss something, and I feel like that's what I missed: transitioning to a living facility, and then going back into the Free World. . . . You have to have that support system." With Haynes's help and the jail volunteers—among them Haynes's mother, who teaches exercise and Bible study—the women are taught structure and discipline, while facing their addictions head-on.

I asked if anyone had been locked up before.

Nearly everyone raised their hands.

While proper placement, diagnosis, programs, and living situations were supposed to be built into the DNA of the direct-supervision model, it seemed there were issues outside the jail's control. Haynes told me the high recidivism rate is due to a lack of housing on the outside. "I just wish we had more available places for women," Haynes sighed. "Women [lacking housing] is the hardest and biggest issue that we need to tackle as a community. The state's strict drugs laws, coupled with lack of transitional housing . . . it's easy to go right back through the revolving door, back into the system."

Donald Ansley led me inside the Garland County's "sick unit," which was used for discipline, closed custody, administrative confinement, and housing for people suffering from severe mental health issues. Unlike the other dorms at Garland, every cell in the sick unit was locked and occupied. When Ansley and I entered, there was no one playing basketball, no card dealing, no snack-time chatter—just someone locked up, banging and hollering.

"Woman entering," Ansley said into the empty living-room area.

The banging stopped.

The living room had no couches, just three small tables without chairs and the CO seated at his desk. Around him were two levels of cells, each containing a mattress, pillow, toilet, access to water, and a person. The CO controlled everything inside, including the lights. If occupants behave, they get one hour of recreational time per day, but the rec yard is much smaller. Visitation rights are viewed as a privilege and can just as easily be revoked. The security is tighter, the materials much harder. For the cost of building these high-security cells—using the costly steel options sold at justice architecture trade events—an entire direct-supervision dorm could be built.

"Some days an inmate requires 100 percent of your attention. That's a bad day. That's a busy day," the CO told me. Behind us, an incarcerated man was crouched down in his cell, listening through the bean hole. He was in his early forties, with long hair and a tattooed stomach, and he wore a towel wrapped around his waist. He'd been there for four months. The officer explained there was nowhere else he could live. Those who have been court ordered to the state mental hospital can't go because the hospital has no available beds. The jail is the only place they could go, he said.

"We weren't designed to handle mental health." Ansley shook his head. "Jails across America are becoming mental institutions. Sixty to seventy percent of people arrested have some kind of mental health issue."

This is not unique to Garland County, or even to Arkansas. While corrections funding has shot up around the nation, there also has been wide defunding of mental hospitals and broad deinstitutionalization. Jails have become home to some of the nation's most vulnerable populations. Ansley was correct. An article in a magazine of the American Psychological Association said that 64 percent of people in America's jails have reported mental health concerns. Jails in New York City, Los Angeles, and Chicago have become some of the country's largest psychiatric-care providers. The rising number of people suffering from mental health issues who are stuck in the nation's jails presents distinct ethical, structural, and financial issues.

"The prosecutor's office can be our number one enemy in a direct-supervision facility," one of the staff members told me. "A lot of them are not efficient; they're not timely, they don't care about mental health. I have a guy who's been here four and half years, still not sentenced! A felony conviction takes years. It's a nightmare. A lot of people here don't even know who their attorney is. They see them once at court. It's terrible."

As Ansley walked me back down Main Street, he nodded to the other end of the corridor. He said Garland County was planning to add another long hallway to accommodate a larger population. "This place is filled with substance-abuse and mentally ill folks. We don't have anywhere else to put them," one CO told me.

"We wouldn't need more jail space if the mentally ill were in the right place," Ansley said. "There's nothing we can do."

———

Since the Garland County Detention Center opened, Ansley said, the incarcerated population has doubled. The staff attributes this to draconian drug laws, a lack of housing and reentry programs, and a slow legal system. I realized how much easier it can be to talk about design than it is to talk about what society is missing and how we can address people's needs. It seems that no matter how well a jail is designed, how prime its location, how competent or understanding its staff, people are being funneled into captivity for reasons beyond the jail's control. Soon, there'll be even more jail beds.

When I caught up with Greg Cook again, I told him about my own experience at the jail he'd designed. The architect was crestfallen. "Those cells were not designed to hold anybody even *near* that amount of time," he said. This, sadly, is a common occurrence in America's jails, even in direct supervision.

Cook then said he'd made a big change in his life.

He'd come a long way since his early days in justice architecture, when he was honored as an "Emerging Professional" and had plenty of optimism and goals to change how we view justice. Over the years, he'd developed keen insights into America's criminal-justice system. He'd also found there to be concerning issues in his field.

"I left my firm in August," Cook confessed. One of the industry's most invested, progressive architects left what he called "the corporate corrections market." He didn't like the way the industry was headed. Some of the mega firms, he saw, were biased and deeply flawed.

"What happened?" I asked.

"A lot of people left HDR because it changed. There were people there I disagreed with, and they had more political power," he explained. "There had been some frustration with HDR's justice practice leadership, and I was concerned about how my career was progressing." This justice architect no longer wanted to design spaces just made for confinement.

I thought about those on the ground I'd talked to—mainly the incarcerated, the COs, the cops, and those recently released from jail. They all said society needs more programs, affordable housing, mental health support, addiction counseling, transition services, and healing processes. New jails weren't the answer.

SEVEN

The Bureaucrats

N*ew York City's top brass* begged to differ. Wanting to hear high-ranking bureaucrats' thoughts on the new jails, I reached out for interviews. By the nature of government, this presented its own challenges. High-ranking officials can be hard to pin down, partly because they're guarded by their press agents—the gatekeepers who vet the media requests and decide who officials will speak to and how. These press agents—some journalists in their former lives—support their organizations' agendas, devise strategic rhetoric and talking points, and disseminate information to the press and public. If a journalist secures an in-person interview, a press agent is invariably present, monitoring every word spoken by their charge.

The city's Department of Design and Construction (DDC) was spearheading the Borough-Based Jails design and construction. With an estimated $15 billion budget, the DDC has led such construction projects as the Queens Botanical Garden, MoMA PS1's visitors' center, and the reconstructed Times Square Plaza and Columbus Circle. This agency seemed like a good place to start, and I let the DDC's top press agent know I was covering the program for *Architectural Digest*. After a month of skillful gymnastics, I clenched a three-for-one deal: an interview with three high-ranking bureaucrats at the DDC. If anyone would know about the design and goals of the BBJ program, it was them.

The DDC is a crucial part of the city bureaucracy, but it is also fairly new. This agency was formed in 1996, when the city pulled together construction arms from various maintenance and building agencies and put them under one roof. Today, the DDC offices reside in a redeveloped industrial neighborhood in Long Island City, in the borough of Queens. Participating in the interview was First Deputy Commissioner Jamie Torres Springer, Deputy Commissioner for Public Buildings Thomas Foley, and Director of Public Building Michaela Metcalfe. They were part of a delegation that visited Europe to study best practices in prison design. As soon as the interview kicked off, the DDC officials seemed determined to show their enthusiasm for the Borough-Based Jails program.

"This is a huge program, not only across the state, but worldwide!" Foley exclaimed. There was heavy focus from the team on positioning the new jails as "civic buildings" rather than detention facilities. The design of the jails would have to "allow for movement" and have the "ability to provide light," while "providing security," they said, sounding much like the folks at the Garland County Detention Center. The new jails would also have to offer visiting areas and rehabilitative spaces, and use "normative" design, a term used frequently in justice architecture to signal they were treating humans likes humans. (I remember Greg

Cook saying *normative* is his least favorite word. "I think a lot of architects use it to imply that their designs are somehow aligned with what we would consider 'normal'—colors, moveable furnishings, artwork. . . . I've always thought it was BS—put all the color you want in a room and it's still not 'normal' for 40 grown men [or women] to occupy a space like that.")

When I asked about how these new jails would work in the city's dense neighborhoods, Metcalfe chimed in. "The new jails need to be responsive to their urban context and surrounding neighborhoods," she said. "We want to make sure what we're putting in place will be reflective of the community," she added, without explaining how. She followed up by saying they want "to create a humane environment for those who visit, those who are detained and work there, and those who live in the community. It's all equally important."

"Do you think that the design can affect behavior and influence recidivism?" I asked.

"Absolutely!" Foley responded. "I always thought so and was reaffirmed when we visited other facilities [on the trip to Europe]. Walking through various sites in Amsterdam and Norway, seeing the materials used, why they used them, and the people working in the facilities; it reaffirms our position and what we're looking for and that we need to have excellent design inside and out."

"One of the things driving this program is that environment drives behavior," Springer offered. "Design is one of the ways that we'll achieve our criminal justice goals. We're moving away from Rikers Island. Part of that is the isolation makes it much more difficult to be rehabilitative and thrive in the criminal justice system in New York City."

"But can someone thrive behind bars?" I asked.

"We're creating an environment that's therapeutic, normative, and supports rehabilitation." Springer repeated the well-worn lines.

After the interview, I reached out to the DDC's press agent with follow-up questions, but the agent was reluctant to answer further questions. He said he felt the agency hadn't received enough ink in my last article.

He also pointed out that the city's next mayor could cancel the entire BBJ program.

The Mayor's Office of Criminal Justice advises New York City's mayor on matters of criminal justice, and also launches programs, task forces, and strategies to help reduce violence and incarceration. For instance, this city agency launched the Domestic Violence Task Force, the Office of Crime Victim Supports, and transitional housing programs, partnering with nonprofits including the Fortune Society and Housing Works. The Mayor's Office of Criminal Justice had also been working closely with the DDC and the Department of Correction to implement the Borough-Based Jails program.

In charge of the Mayor's Office of Criminal Justice was Elizabeth Glazer, the high-ranking bureaucrat who'd stood beside Mayor de Blasio at City Hall in 2017 when he announced the Rikers Island closure. As its executive director, Glazer was seen as an "architect" of the plan to close Rikers. A Harvard University and Columbia Law School graduate, Glazer was a formidable force in government, clerking in her early career for then–U.S. circuit court judge Ruth Bader Ginsburg, and later working as a federal prosecutor. Under Governor Andrew Cuomo, she served as deputy secretary for public safety for New York State. Then, in 2015, Mayor de Blasio appointed Glazer as executive director of the Mayor's Office of Criminal Justice and his most senior criminal-justice policy adviser. She strategized ways to safely decrease the city's incarcerated population, as well as serving as cochair of the Justice Implementation Task Force for the BBJ program. After weeks of negotiation and scheduling back-and-forth, I nailed an in-person interview.

It was a cold, misty morning when I walked down to lower Manhattan to the David N. Dinkins Manhattan Municipal Building, one of the world's largest government office buildings. Residing at 1 Centre Street, this enormous limestone building presides over downtown and was one of the world's earliest skyscrapers; it was also one of the last buildings erected as part of the City Beautiful movement of the early 1900s. Standing alongside the Woolworth Building, City Hall, St. Paul's Chapel, and many of Manhattan's courthouses, it was created at the turn of the century by the iconic architecture firm McKim Mead & White. Today it houses 2,000 employees from a dozen municipal agencies, as well as the city comptroller, the public advocate, and the Manhattan borough president.

The confluence of Beaux-Arts, Roman Imperial, and French and Italian Renaissance architectural styles belies the building's dreary interior. Upon entering, visitors are in a security room with peeling plaster walls, and they shove their belongings through an

X-ray machine, then walk through a metal detector. Once they have been security-cleared, visitors are shuffled into a marble-clad hallway lit with stinging fluorescent lights, the mosaic floors dull and scuffed over time. I rode one of the building's 33 elevators and reached the 10th floor, where I was ushered into a conference room. Elizabeth Glazer and her Chief of Public Affairs, Colby Hamilton, awaited me.

Glazer greeted me with a kind hello and apologized for the aesthetics of the room, noting with a smile that I must be accustomed to more chic interiors, as a contributor to *Architectural Digest*. She beckoned me over to the bay windows facing west and pointed out a row of turn-of-the-century landmarks standing proud, like soldiers. She named her favorites and remarked on their architectural grandeur before moving on to the reason I'd come to her office.

"It's an amazing story," Glazer gushed. "I think it's an extraordinary, world historic story, actually, because it's certainly about the buildings, but it's about so much more than that." She explained that it would be the biggest public works project in generations, the city's largest justice-reform effort in history, and potentially the country's largest justice-reform effort currently or ever under way. It was a great opportunity: New York City had given itself the liberty to "start from scratch" and to reimagine what a "humane environment" means.

"When we think about the buildings," she proceded, "we think about buildings that match the ambition of the justice transformation that the city is undergoing right now and everything that that means, both about people who work and live and are incarcerated inside the buildings and also how the buildings fit into neighborhoods, and how they, themselves, can be civic assets for people who live in the neighborhoods. And so that notion of how neighborhoods are integrated, how the buildings are integrated into those neighborhoods, is a very important part of this whole effort." She noted that of all the jails she'd visited, she had yet to find another jail built in such dense, urban environments as will be the Borough-Based Jails.

I asked how this program would impact the people on the inside, and what the city was doing about the disproportionate number of people of color incarcerated.

"The numbers have dropped dramatically," Glazer replied, "but this is an issue that goes well beyond simply jails. It's about our justice system and how people become involved in the justice system to begin with. And it's an issue of deep concern for all of us."

Did she think design would make a difference? I asked.

"I think if you built a beautiful building, it was well designed, but that you didn't change anything about what you did inside, that would not be enough. These things have to work in tandem— both the way in which we think about correctional practices and the way in which buildings are constructed," Glazer said.

On their European trip, she noted, the group found two things particularly striking. The first was the consistent philosophy that it is the correction officers' responsibility to prepare incarcerated people for success upon release. The second was an architect's explanation that certain principles had to be integrated into a jail, no matter the location: light and air. Glazer said that the freedom to reimagine the jail system was an enormous and inspiring opportunity for the city.

Again, I asked about the people who were being impacted most directly. Had the office spoken to any incarcerated or formerly incarcerated New Yorkers?

"Mm-hmm, yup," She replied. Glazer straightened up and looked down at the conference table. "One of the most important things for us," she began slowly but confidently, "has been that every aspect of the criminal justice reform effort in the city, whether it has to do with Rikers or other things, is done in partnership with advocacy organizations, [the] formerly incarcerated. That voice is a critical voice, obviously. I think if you had to sum it up in one word, the word would be *dignity*. You want buildings that reflect the dignity of people who are incarcerated, of people who visit, of people who work there, and [of those] who promote that sense of respect inside."

It was a graceful way to dodge the question. These talking points seemed to reveal that no real effort had been made to listen to the very people the city promised to help. The reality is, considering that nearly one in 100 Americans will be incarcerated in their lifetime, we hear relatively few of their voices. As a society we tend to believe that if people get themselves locked up, then they probably don't know what's best for them. Arguably, it can be this sort of thought process that leads to their not be listened to or considered. Formerly incarcerated individuals who are lucky enough to have a platform often have that access because they work at nonprofits and civic organizations, which tend to have their own agendas, press agents, and vested interests.

I cleared my throat and looked into Glazer's eyes. "This might seem pretty basic," I started, "but do you believe it's a good idea to close Rikers? And if so, why?"

The press agent, who'd been reading his phone up until now, flicked his eyes at Glazer, who let out an incredulous laugh.

"That's a curveball question!" She laughed again as she tried to compose herself. "I think, uh, I think about it less as the negative of closing Rikers and more as . . ." she continued, gaining some footing, "the positive of building justice."

Then the conversation jumped to a different track. "I think that since the time Rikers was built in the 1920s, how we conceive of keeping ourselves safe, what the roles of prison and the justice system are, what the reach of the justice system is into the lives of New Yorkers has changed utterly. And so we now have an opportunity in the context of this major shift, in the way in which the justice system operates, to also create facilities that reflect that shift, meaning buildings that have light and air, that are well designed, that have room for programming space and education, that have room for civic activities in the building, as well as space for people who are incarcerated. These are all things that are crucial to how we think about the rehabilitative function of the justice system."

Less than a year after our interview, Liz Glazer resigned.

EIGHT
The Neighbors

As *2021 was coming to a close*, Mayor Bill de Blasio seemed to be trying to leave office on a high note. Just days before his departure from his mayoral seat, he made sure to announce the design-build teams selected for what could be his legacy. The names of the construction firms were made public, but the architecture firms were not. I pressed the Department of Design and Construction for the architecture firms' names, and finally the agency agreed to release them. The list included some of the biggest and most glamorous firms: HDR, HOK/CGL Design JV, Perkins Eastman, DLR Group, STV Incorporated/Morris Adjmi Architects, and Urbahn Architects/Cetra-Ruddy.

Rikers Island, meanwhile, was being called a "humanitarian crisis." Sixteen men died that year on Rikers. The question of a federal takeover loomed. The oldest jail on Rikers—the Art Deco institution—had changed hands from the Department of Correction to the Department of Citywide Administration Services, signaling the city's intention to keep moving forward with closing every jail on Rikers, step by step. New York City's next mayor would inherit this byzantine reform effort.

Just after midnight on January 1, 2022, New York City's new mayor, Eric Adams, stood on a stage in Times Square. After the ball dropped and Frank Sinatra's "New York, New York" serenaded the crowds, the inauguration ceremony began. Adams, wearing a crisp navy suit with a pocket square and a mask looped around his wrist, became the city's 110th mayor and its second Black mayor in its history. Adams raised his right hand and the audience cheered, confetti floating down the billboard and neon-lit streets.

A new year and a new era had begun.

Born in Brownsville, Brooklyn, Adams came from a working-class family and became New York's first mayor in over 70 years who had come from law enforcement.[*] A 1984 graduate of the New York City Police Academy, with the second-highest average in his class, Adams served in the NYPD and the transit police for two decades, during which time he advocated for Black officers and spoke against police brutality. After retiring as an NYPD captain in 2006, he served in the New York State Senate, representing the 20th Senate District, in Brooklyn, before advancing to Brooklyn borough president. On his mayoral campaign trail, Adams had positioned himself as a blue-collar mayor who would be tough on crime. When he was questioned about the city's new jails program, he sent mixed signals. He agreed that Rikers Island needed to close, but he said that the jail locations would be

---

[*] This was since William O'Dwyer, who became a cop in law school, and was mayor from 1946 to 1950.

subject to more discussion. During one mayoral forum, he was more specific about the jail slated to replace the Tombs in lower Manhattan. "I do not support building the jail. I believe we've dumped on the Chinatown community long enough," he said at an event hosted by the Asian American Federation.

In Adams's first month as mayor, conditions at Rikers were as bad as ever. In January 2022, hundreds of incarcerated people staged a hunger strike to protest the awful conditions at the jail, including the lack of heat during the freezing winter months, no hot water in some units, inconsistent medical care, and problems with issues with security and sanitation.

Crime, meanwhile, continued to be a hot-button topic in the waning years of the pandemic. The conversations about incarceration—in New York City, in particular—became nearly inescapable, and the issues Adams seemed to prioritize concerned activists and reform-minded constituents. With a tough-on-crime retired cop now in charge, some wondered if the city's jail population could really be reduced to 3,544 as de Blasio had promised. It seemed unlikely to skeptics, including New York City Department of Correction commissioner Louis Molina, who told City Council members that the department would not reach this number by 2027. "I don't see [us] being at 3,300 in less than four years, if nothing else changes with the administration and adjudication of the administration of justice at the court levels," Molina said. "I think if Rikers has to close we have to think about where does the balance of that people go."

As Adams settled in at Gracie Mansion, news emerged of more concrete plans to build the new jails. It was spring 2022, and preparations to demolish the Tombs were under way, signaling that Adams was now on board. The city had quietly removed all the incarcerated people. Inside, the Tombs were silent as the grave. Cranes and construction crews would soon be the jail complex's occupants.

On April 11, 2022, protestors—many of them neighbors of the jail—formed a blockade in Chinatown where the Tombs rests. Former presidential candidate Andrew Yang's wife, Evelyn, was among the protestors, and she was arrested by NYPD officers, her hands zip-tied. She admonished Mayor Adams to the local press and cameras. "How dare you make this promise . . . then turn your back on them!"

"Hell no!" protestors shouted.

"No new jail!"

Chants echoed down the street as NYPD officers stood by the two edifices that make up the Tombs: the Brutalist-style North Tower, which opened in 1990, and the Art Deco–style South Tower adjacent to the criminal courthouse. These towers were connected by a raised pedestrian bridge, which passersby could walk under to get from Tribeca to Chinatown. Though the Tombs is where these two neighborhoods meet, each neighborhood's residents had different feelings about their correctional neighbor.

Tribeca, once a center for the cotton and textile industry, was transformed when artists planted their roots there in the 1960s and 1970s, converting abandoned merchant buildings into live/work studios. Decades later, after real estate giants had seized the open lofts and demanded top rental dollars, Tribeca is now one of the city's most affluent neighborhoods, home to the posh

Greenwich Hotel, the velvet-rope nightclub Paul's Baby Grand, the Tribeca Film Festival, and celebrities like Taylor Swift, Kevin Love, and Jake Gyllenhaal. The art world marked its territory here, too, with galleries like David Zwirner's 52 Walker, Andrew Kreps, PPOW, Bortolami, Luhring Augustine, and James Cohan moving into those relics of the defunct textile industry. Walking down the cobbled streets, with shopfronts displaying contemporary art and $1,200 denim, a person is more likely to pass fashionable mothers with children and bankers power-lunching al fresco than any indication of mass incarceration. When I asked around the neighborhood about residents' thoughts on the new jails program and the demolition of the Tombs (or the official name, the Manhattan Detention Complex), most people I talked to didn't know a jail was just down the road.

"There's a jail near here?" someone responded when asked. Another was even more confused: "Is it Manhattan's only jail?" Only a few were aware of the initiative; those who did know were suspicious, calling it a "crackpot idea that de Blasio started" or "a PR stunt." Most consider this to be an issue beyond the borders of their neighborhood—something "over there" that doesn't impact them. "I heard a mural was going to be demolished. That's as much as I can say," offered a gallery staffer, referring to the work of artist Richard Haas, which would likely be collateral damage in the dismantling. (Artists had sued the city in an attempt to save their works at the Tombs, citing the Visual Artists Rights Act of 1990, but in May 2022, a judge denied their request, saying the artists couldn't prove that their artwork outweighed the public interest.)

Heading east down Tribeca's White Street, the cast-iron

façades spread like an accordion, but the road stops dead at the Tombs. At this site, there is a long history of jails: the original Egyptian Revival–style jail was designed by none other than John Haviland, the architect of Eastern State Penitentiary. That jail was eventually demolished, making away for several other jail renditions, until the current towers were erected. Now, fences and signs posted by the city's Department of Design and Construction block all street traffic.

In Chinatown, just east of the Tombs, a microeconomy thrives on Baxter Street, where a row of bail-bond shops with blue, red, and green awnings advertise their services. "Get out of jail fast!" "Large or small, we write them all!" "*Fianzas!*" (Spanish for "bail.") While Manhattan's Chinatown is America's largest, it's also in one of the city's poorest neighborhoods, with 26.5 percent of its residents living in poverty. This immigrant neighborhood formed in the mid-nineteenth and early twentieth centuries during a dynamic period of Asian immigration. Despite fervent racism and the 1882 Chinese Exclusion Act, the area experienced a boom, attracting people from all over the world. With higher-income residents later moving into the surrounding neighborhoods, developers began nosing in. Now dotted with dim sum spots, outdoor fish and produce markets, restaurants, underground bars, and small tenement buildings (some flat-roofed and others with Chinese pagoda-style porch roofs), the area's rent prices began soaring, leaving older residents with minimal options for subsidized housing and affordable rent. While Tribeca residents have the luxury to be distanced from the jail, those in Chinatown literally live in the shadow of the Tombs.

Many Chinatown residents gather at the Tombs' next-door

neighbor, a nineteenth-century park designed by Central Park's codesigner Calvert Veaux. Columbus Park differs from the manicured greenspaces of Tribeca. Here, people sleep on benches along the curved walkways, play mahjong, drink bottles of beer hidden in brown bags at cement picnic tables, and play cards under makeshift tents of blue tarp. The smell of sunbaked urine in the Astroturf permeates the air. On any given morning, you might see a woman watering the hydrangeas by the basketball courts, and another practicing tai chi, as garbage bins overflow with rotten food and other waste. Columbus Park habitués have unparalleled views of the Tombs, and they have a lot to say about the jail. Many residents here strongly oppose the city's BBJ program. Some are elderly residents of the nearby senior living center, and they are concerned about the pollution, noise, and health hazards during the years-long construction. Others feel the city is neglecting their neighborhood. They need affordable housing and health clinics, not a massive, high-rise jail to replace the current two towers.

This isn't the first time Chinatown residents have confronted the city's split political priorities. During Mayor Ed Koch's reign, in 1982, the second tower of the Tombs was slated for construction, in response to a federal court order forcing the city to close some of Rikers Island's outdated cells. Protests and rallies flooded the streets. "We need housing, not new jails!" people cried. Neighbors needed schools, daycare centers, and jobs. Yet jail construction moved forward. Now, decades later, the city was going to build yet another jail, despite the neighbors' protests. Chinatown's residents refused to back down.

In 2018, about 300 local business owners and organizations banded together to form a group called Neighbors United

Below Canal (NUBC), which has since expanded to thousands of stakeholders. The purpose of NUBC was to speak with a unified voice against the new jail. In February 2020, NUBC joined forces with the local nonprofit American Indian Community House, and together they filed a lawsuit against the city to stop the new jail. In the filing, the groups accused the city of failing to reach out to residents who would be affected by the new jail construction, and of violating its land-use procedure.

NUBC cofounder Jan Lee, a general contractor and property owner, is adamant about not letting history repeat itself. For the last 96 years, Lee's family has owned two Chinatown tenement buildings. "People said we're just a bunch of NIMBY people," Lee said.

NIMBY, or Not In My Backyard, are residents who oppose new development—such as jails, affordable housing, safe houses, and other institutions—because they feel it would be unsafe, decrease property values, or invite less-than-desirable neighbors. Some accuse NIMBYists of sacrificing the public good to maintain their status quo. The late George Carlin aptly captures this attitude in his 1992 comedy set *Jammin' in New York*: "People don't want any kind of social help located anywhere near them. You try and open up a halfway house, you try to open up a rehab center for drugs or alcohol . . . people say, 'Not in my backyard!' People don't want anything near them, especially if it might help somebody else, part of the great American spirit of generosity we're always told about . . . even if it's something they believe in, even if it's something they think society needs, like prisons. . . . Everybody wants more prisons. . . . That's the new answer to all of our problems: Lock the motherfuckers up. . . . They say, 'Build more prisons! But not here.'"

Critics of NIMBYism say this mentality helps maintain a level of residential segregation. "Because individuals and families in need of affordable housing are disproportionately people of color," the Shriver Center on Poverty Law reported in 2018, "local control over affordable housing development serves as a present-day proxy for racial discrimination." An example reigns in the liberal state of Connecticut. During the last 20 years, over three dozen Connecticut towns used exclusionary zoning requirements to block unwanted private apartment and duplex construction. The state's southwest region has the nation's widest gap between rich and poor, where Black and Hispanic people are confined to America's most segregated neighborhoods.

"People would accuse us of being selfish, rich, elitist, and racist, that we care more about parking than we do about Black and Brown people. I've heard that many times," Jan Lee continued. He blames the major criminal-justice foundations for stirring up the NIMBY narrative. "These accusers, mainly from these big foundations, are operating under this suffocating blanket of morality." The big nonprofits and the city, he believes, routinely dismiss his community's needs and steamroll them to make way for yet another jail.

This is not unusual. Part of America's legacy is defined by power players ignoring the needs of lower-income minority communities. Throughout its history, America has built industrial developments, freeways, and chemical and power plants in the backyards of marginalized communities, infiltrating neighborhoods with no regard for the social or economic impact. One major example of this is the urban renewal movement, where swaths of lower-income communities of color were removed from their homes to make way for new development. Perhaps this is no better embodied than in the public projects led by Robert Moses, one of history's most powerful, divisive urban planners, who reshaped midcentury New York City. During Moses's reign, new legislation was passed allowing the city to use eminent domain—the power of the government to take private property in the name of public good. "The idea was to enlist the private sector to build affordable housing that would help the city retain its middle-class population, who were increasingly departing for the suburbs," writes Anthony Flint in his book, *Wrestling with Moses*. Moses became infamous for his use of eminent domain to remove hundreds of thousands of people from their homes.

One of Moses's first and most notorious housing projects was the large-scale housing development Stuyvesant Town, a complex of 35 buildings on 80 acres just north of Manhattan's East Village. Developed by the Metropolitan Life Insurance Company, the project involved evicting the area's mostly lower-income residents, citing eminent domain. They then built Stuyvesant Town for whites only, embodying the racism entrenched in America's urban-renewal movement. Moses continued this trend throughout a career that spanned much of the mid-twentieth century.

Under the federal Housing Act of 1949, a program known as Title I supposedly ensured former residents places to live, but thousands of minority families and lower-income people lost their homes nevertheless. The former residents had no say in the matter, had nowhere to go, and received no compensation for their uprooting. Scores of lower-income, mostly minority communities were destroyed to make way for modernist structures for the middle class and to build "the modern city" in the name of urban renewal.

Moses's blueprint helped shape the land-development ethos that followed for decades. Later urban-renewal practitioners—influenced heavily by Moses and the modernist architectural movement—razed lower-income communities in Chicago, Boston, Philadelphia, and beyond, and erected austere, modernist monoliths and towers in their place, with little local input or consideration.

This power play persists today, where lower-income neighborhoods of color become "sacrifice zones." Aside from these communities being cleared for new development, they also have been neighbors to new chemical and power plants, landfills, incinerators, and highways, causing these communities to suffer greater incidences of toxicity and pollution and higher mortality rates. "Minority, low-income, and indigenous populations frequently bear a disproportionate burden of environmental harms and adverse health outcomes, including the development of heart or lung diseases, such as asthma and bronchitis, increased susceptibility to respiratory and cardiac symptoms, greater numbers of emergency room visits and hospital admissions, and premature deaths," the U.S. Environmental Protection Agency said in a report about power plants built in rural communities. In majority-Black communities, the industrial air pollution that causes cancer is more than double that of majority-white communities. Since the 1970s, it's been reported that Black Americans have experienced increases in asthma morbidity because of exposure to certain environmental factors, including air pollutants and allergens.

In Chinatown, residents were sick and tired of New York City building jails in their community: the city had invested in the carceral cycle for far too long, and it wasn't working. The city was now about to spend $2 billion to replace the standing towers of the Tombs, when this community needed affordable housing, programs, and community investment to help *prevent* crime. Anything else, Jan Lee told me, was sending a clear message to the young people of Chinatown: "Your future is in this building. . . . We haven't recognized historically that we're not good at jails. It's never been about the structure of the jail. We just keep reinventing with a new concrete structure. It's time to start looking at what we can do in communities."

Iakowi:he'ne' (Melissa) Oakes, who served as executive director of the coplaintiff American Indian Community House, shared similar feelings with Lee. Oakes lived between Manhattan and Akwesasne Mohawk Territory, on the border of New York State and Canada. She was keenly aware of the Tombs, not just because the jail was near her office and she kept up with the news, but also because she'd been incarcerated there once herself.

While driving her Cadillac SUV, she was pulled over by an NYPD cop, who said the tint on her windows was too dark. When Oakes handed over her license, she didn't realize it had been suspended (for having not paid a speeding ticket and a seatbelt violation). "He arrested me on the spot," she recalled. The young mother of two was tossed into a holding cell. Later that night, she was locked in a room with many other women at the Tombs, where she spent the night in the freezing cold. "It was April and I was wearing capris and a little light jacket. . . . It snowed that night. I was in a concrete box and they left all the windows open. It was torture. There were no blankets, just 200 other women and thin mats, like yoga mats. I didn't have a mat and one woman shared hers with me. We laid back-to-back to stay warm." The next day, she went to court and was released.

"They treated us like animals," she said, clearly still haunted by the experience. "It's not natural or healthy to lock someone up. It causes harm through threats and control. It's wasteful to that person and everyone around that person." The experience was a factor in her opposing new jails, though in general she opposes colonial carceral systems. It's "more about chattel and control over people," mainly, she said, people of color. "Being a person who is federally recognized as a member of a tribal nation—we're a sovereign nation, so to deal with any other system . . . they're so emboldened to not even care, these people running these systems." She added that a jail "would be bad feng shui. There would be Shar in the middle of the community, it's bad energy and toxic."

When the lawyers for Neighbors United Below Canal reached out to the American Indian Community House to get involved in their lawsuit, Oakes invited the lawyers into her office and agreed to get on board, believing that it was inherently connected to the mission and outlook of her people. "As a

Mohawk and a woodlands people of the Northeast, everything is sacred. . . . But everything has been assimilated into a colonial, capitalist society, where nothing is sacred and everything is a commodity and about control. . . . We are wild beings, we're not caged chickens and cows."

While the neighbors won their case against the city—on both their technical land-use and their quality-of-life arguments—their victory was ultimately thwarted. In March 2021, the New York State Appeals Court overturned the ruling, saying, "the scoping process in this case was not arbitrary and capricious, affected by an error of law, or in violation of lawful procedure," and that the environmental review had adequately considered the health risks of the new construction. The four-judge panel unanimously ruled in favor of New York City. The jail in lower Manhattan could move forward.

Neighbors were once again infuriated, and more and more people were getting on board. Architects, too, were questioning their role in America's criminal justice system. There was one architect's name in particular I kept hearing. He lived in San Francisco, and for years has been urging his peers to examine their ethical boundaries with design.

The architect's name was Raphael Sperry, and he was a prison abolitionist.

NINE

The Prison Abolitionists

For the last 20 years, Raphael Sperry has been a firebrand advocating for change, particularly in the justice-architecture community. After graduating from the Yale School of Architecture in the early 2000s, the young architect with rimmed glasses and devil-may-care curls ventured west to find his future. Settling in San Francisco, a historic hotbed of American social movements, Sperry discovered his passion for activism.

When the United States invaded Iraq in 2003, antiwar rallies erupted around the globe, and the Bay Area once again became a newsbreaking center of protest.* Sperry helped plan a protest, and on the second day, he and his fellow musicians in the Brass Liberation Orchestra headed to San Francisco's East Cut neighborhood, where they jammed outside the headquarters of the Bechtel Corporation, one of the largest and most politically

---

* The number of civilians who died in the Iraq War is unclear, but it is estimated to be between 184,382 and 207,156, according to the Costs of War Project, based at the Watson Institute for International and Public Affairs, at Brown University.

connected construction companies in the world. Many protestors saw Bechtel, along with Lockheed Martin, Chevron, and Halliburton, as war profiteers, part of the "military industrial complex," a constellation of individuals and businesses that have vested interests in waging war. The Brass Liberation Orchestra helped keep the tempo in the East Cut.

"No blood for oil . . . again!"

"We don't want your fucking war!"

Some protestors played music, some flashed peace signs, others held picket signs or sat cross-legged facing SWAT teams. Soon, police officers closed in and arrested the musicians, bringing them to a temporary overflow station at a nearby waterfront pier. Hours later, Sperry was released, the charges eventually dropped (the cops held Sperry's bass drum for a week as "evidence").

This wouldn't be the last time Raphael Sperry was arrested. The next year, in his hometown of New York City, Sperry joined tens of thousands of people protesting at the Republican National Convention. Over the course of four days in late August, hundreds of groups organized marches, rallies, performances, and speeches against the impending renomination of President George W. Bush to the party's ticket. Sperry was one of 1,800 detainees arrested by the NYPD and transported to jails around the city. In Sperry's case, he was taken to the Tombs, where he spent one harrowing night in jail.

Though he had anticipated the possibility of arrest, Sperry recalls how deeply it affected him. "Being in jail is a very powerless, lonely, and scary experience, even for someone as privileged as I am, with the confidence that I'd done nothing wrong," Sperry told me. "Knowing you'll be able to sue later does not give you much of a feeling of protection when you're held in a cage with people shouting at you, pushing you around, and keeping you under their thumb." The next day, Sperry was released. The National Lawyers Guild got in touch with Sperry and many others arrested during the protest. They brought a lawsuit against the city, and several years later, Sperry received a settlement for wrongful arrest.

He was beginning to see parallels between America's military industrial complex and its prison industrial complex. "I think America uses violence as an instrument of policy. . . . We had a war abroad and a war at home," Sperry told me. The architect turned his activism inward and challenged the nation's prison industrial complex, in which companies and leaders were profiting by incarcerating people, many of them untried. The best way he could drive awareness, he decided, was to work within a space he knew well.

Sperry started prompting professionals in the architecture community to question the ethics of designing America's prisons and jails. "Prisons are a really deep and powerful example of how architects and engineers are connected to systems of oppression," he said. Sperry became a fighting force, galvanizing support for this cause, both within the architecture community and with citizens at large. His first major step was to join the board at the San Francisco–based nonprofit organization Architects/Designers/Planners for Social Responsibility (ADPSR), an antiwar group promoting nuclear disarmament. Founded in 1981, ADPSR has expanded its efforts to include socially responsible development. The organization is well respected, having been

honored by the American Institute of Architects and other official organizations. They offered Sperry a structured way to talk
with architects and designers about prisons, architecture, and
ethics.

In 2004, Sperry and ADPSR launched the Prison Design
Boycott for Alternatives to Incarceration, a campaign that asked
architects and design professionals to vow to stop designing
prisons and jails. "The Prison Boycott turned the critique of
militarism inwards to call out prisons and jails as the architectural embodiment of the domestic war on poor people of color,"
Sperry wrote in his 2018 posting on the Now What?! website.
Other campaigns and boycotts followed, championed by Sperry
and his colleagues at ADPSR. Thousands of people signed petitions.

Prominent architects and thinkers, such as *New York Times*
architecture critic Michael Kimmelman and the late architect
Michael Sorkin, were on board. Sorkin argued that architects
should not design institutions that cause harm. "The supermax
represents the almost complete abandonment of the idea of
rehabilitation. . . . Supermax prisons are factories of recidivism,
rage, madness and suicide," Sorkin wrote in *The Nation*, calling out justice architecture firms, like DLR Group, Arrington
Watkins, KMD, and Schenkel Schultz. The prison boom, which
launched under President Ronald Reagan, was "one of the ugly
legacies of the Gipper, Papa Bush and Bill Clinton, a racist project pure and simple," Sorkin declared.

"Architecture is never nonpolitical: It always reinforces a
set of social relations, whether within the family or between the

ruler and the ruled," Sorkin said in an interview for the journal *Man and Space*.

Though Sperry wasn't the first architect to draw attention to this, he is one of the better-known, modern-day architects to help spark change. Support for his cause rose through the 2000s, and in 2014, the ADPSR took its biggest stance yet. It launched a petition demanding that the American Institute of Architects (AIA) prohibit its members from designing execution chambers and spaces for prolonged solitary confinement. Those spaces were specifically created for death and torture, they argued, and violated human rights.

The AIA balked.

ADPSR persisted, bringing multiple petitions to architecture's main trade association, but over and over again the AIA dismissed them. The association held that it was not in their purview to decide what architects could and could not design. In a 2019 published advisory opinion, the AIA said, "The design of an execution chamber in the United States does not, in and of itself, constitute conduct in wanton disregard of the rights of others. . . . On the contrary, it reflects conduct that is sanctioned by society in those jurisdictions where capital punishment has been adopted as the law of the land."

Sperry spoke on panel discussions, wrote op-eds, did interviews, and became a fixture in the justice architecture community, whether others in the field liked it or not. He attended justice architecture conferences and trade events. In 2012, he went to an American Association for Justice (AAJ) conference at a Toronto hotel, where outside, locals were protesting construction of a new jail. They said that what the community had really needed was a shelter and an HIV treatment center. Sperry spoke with the locals beforehand and received a statement of their concerns. At the AAJ conference, during the Q and A portion of a panel discussion on the design and construction of the new Toronto Remand Center (Canadian for "jail"), Sperry stood and read the statement to the audience, a mostly male, mostly white, mostly over-40 crowd.

They booed him.

In 2020, there was renewed outrage about racism, inequality, and so-called justice in America. The deaths of George Floyd, Breonna Taylor, and Ahmaud Arbery ignited Black Lives Matter and Defund the Police protests. The wave finally broke, and the discussion went mainstream. Demands mounted for architects to stop designing prisons and jails. In June 2020, Kimmelman drummed up more attention with his *New York Times* piece supporting Sperry's beliefs: "Architects should not contribute their expertise to the most egregious aspects of a system that commits exceptional violence against African-Americans and other minorities. The least the American Institute of Architects can do now is agree."

Still, the AIA didn't budge.

―――

Sperry's efforts are part of a larger, growing movement called prison abolition. This established philosophy believes that prisons and jails need to be dismantled and a new paradigm of justice be built. "[Our belief in prison abolition] grew from watching, experiencing, and opposing decades of reliance on concrete and steel cages as catch-all solutions to social problems," wrote long-time abolition advocate Ruth Wilson Gilmore, with James Kilgore, for the Marshall Project. "We want a society that centers on freedom and justice instead of profit and punishment."

Abolitionists believe the system needs to be dismantled and replaced with new supportive systems and structures. "Abolitionists, therefore, share an idea—a vision—more than a structure: a future in which vital needs like housing, education, and health care, are met, allowing people to live safe and fulfilled lives—without the need for prisons," writes John Washington in *The Nation*.

Modern-day abolition took root in the United States in the 1960s, growing alongside the civil rights movement, when discussions about the justice system, policing, and carceral conditions became a focus of those advocating for equality and human rights. Instead of reforming prisons and jails, some saw a need for a new form of justice. In 1970, a young Black professor named Angela Davis landed on the FBI's Ten Most Wanted Fugitives List after a weapon registered in her name was used in a California courtroom-hostage situation, where people were killed. After being arrested and charged with three capital offenses, Davis spent 16 months in a San Francisco Bay Area jail—often in solitary confinement—awaiting trial. While she had advocated for prison reform, once inside, she experienced a visceral understanding of America's criminal justice system. In 1972, she was acquitted. She became a leader of the prison-abolition movement.

Today, Davis is internationally renowned for her work advocating against prisons and jails. Davis is a distinguished professor emerita at the University of California, Santa Cruz, and she has lectured in all 50 states, as well as around the world. In 1997, Davis, alongside Ruth Wilson Gilmore, Rose Braz, and other abolitionists, cofounded the abolition group Critical Resistance, in Oakland, California, with the goal of forming a mass abolition movement and opposing new jail and prison construction, including New York City's Borough-Based Jails program. Her seminal book, *Are Prisons Obsolete?*, published in 2003, is one of abolition's main texts, where she argues that finding alternatives to prisons and jails is "the most difficult and urgent challenge today."

Make no mistake, prison abolition is not prison reform; these are two distinct philosophies. Both abolitionists and reformists agree that incarceration picked up where slavery left off, fortifying and enabling racism and discrimination in a new way, using the architecture of prisons and jails to conceal it. From here, the two philosophies diverge: Reformists advocate for better prison and jail conditions and police accountability—effectively, for creating better conditions within the current system. Abolitionists believe in building a new system altogether.

To create a new paradigm of justice, it is important the public understands the nature of the system, its history, and the way the system is reinforced. There was a time, Angela Davis reminds us, when slavery and lynching seemed to be "as everlasting as the sun." There were movements and actions that obliterated these seemingly permanent social institutions. Prisons and jails, too, are social institutions that we are trained to accept as part of the American landscape and natural order. The media reinforces this vision, fortifying messages of right and wrong, oversimplifying experiences and impact, and perpetuating stereotypes by portraying the "bad guys" as Black and Brown people. Some of our most celebrated films (such as *The Green Mile* and *The Shawshank Redemption*) and A-list comedies (*Get Hard* and *The Longest Yard*), encourage us to accept prisons as organic-fixtures in society. As Eastern State Penitentiary reminds us, they are not.

Rather than caging people in loud, traumatic environments, segregating them from their social networks and safety nets, an abolitionist might contend that we need to get to the underlying cause of the violence. Oftentimes, violence and harm that are committed stem from deeper structural issues, such as poverty, disenfranchisement, and lack of resources. Violence is complex and requires a granular set of approaches and interventions to make amends, heal, and prevent it from happening again. Many abolitionists understand this firsthand, as many are survivors of violence themselves.

Restorative justice is one alternative approach that abolitionists support. This practice examines the violent act, its implications and effects, and seeks to find a road to repair the harm caused. Rooted in indigenous peacemaking practices, the modern concept of restorative justice was pioneered in the 1970s by American criminologist Howard Zehr. Offenders should "fully account for their behaviors in dialogue with the individual and communities affected by their actions. . . . They must then work with those parties to develop actions to try to repair the damage done as much as possible," says Alex S. Vitale, in John

Washington's *Nation* article. Restorative justice prioritizes the needs of survivors and victims' families, giving them a say in what the road to repair will look like. In today's current legal system, survivors and victims' families are almost never heard (if a case goes to trial, there can be an opportunity for them to speak, but trials are extremely rare). Restorative justice encourages the offender to confront their actions and ultimately make amends to the survivor, the family, and the community.

Common Justice, an organization in Brooklyn, New York, uses a restorative-justice model for those who've experienced and committed harm. The recidivism rate of those who go through Common Justice's program is just 6 percent (as of 2018), compared to the national recidivism rate of 76.6 percent. Based on these numbers, the restorative-justice model proves much more effective than incarceration. Common Justice founder Danielle Sered works with survivors and survivors' families, as well as prosecutors, to redirect violent actors from detention settings to her restorative-justice program. Those who complete the program and fulfill commitments to those they've harmed have their felony charges removed from their records and don't have to serve time in jail or prison.

"People are built to heal," Sered writes in her book *Until We Reckon*, "and when we have information, we are profoundly capable of putting it into the service of our healing. The problem is that survivors rarely have access to such information because every response our systems have created to manage their relationship with the person who hurt them is designed to keep separate rather than to help them come together productively. Survivors do not only want to ask questions. They want to speak and they want their voices heard."

At Sered's program, the offender undergoes an intensive 12- to 15-month intervention, including a violence-intervention program that runs alongside the restorative-justice process. They need to face the consequences and rippling effects of their actions, a fate Sered believes can be more difficult than jail or prison. They work with the survivor, the victim's family, or a proxy, and they unearth why they committed the act in the first place. "If your job is to punish, you just need to punish. If your job is to repair, you need to ask questions and find out the solutions," Sered told me. "When I think about the criminal justice system, if someone burns down your house, the justice system would [figurately] burn down their house in your name. Our goal is to build a new house."

Restorative justice is an example of excarceration, which involves developing alternatives to divert people away from prisons and jails. Longtime abolitionist and organizer Mariame Kaba explains that it's just as much "about dismantling death-making institutions like policing and prisons and surveillance. . . . And creating life-affirming ones, putting resources and investing in things we know do keep people safe: housing, healthcare, schooling, all kinds of other things, living wages . . . those type of investments are what really keep people safe. . . . It's shrinking the legitimacy—shrinking the ideological footprint—of policing within our communities. It's really about taking power away as much as anything from these institutions."

Excarceration is one of the three pillars of abolition's attrition model. The other two pillars are moratorium and decarceration. A moratorium on prisons and jails would stop all construction while communities develop alternatives and violence-prevention plans. Raphael Sperry's work petitioning the AIA could be viewed as part of galvanizing support for a moratorium. This doesn't mean all prisons and jails need to close immediately. "Ultimately, abolition is a practical program of change rooted in how people sustain and improve their lives, cobbling together insights and strategies from disparate, connected struggles," wrote Ruth Wilson Gilmore and James Kilgore for the Marshall Project. "We know we won't bulldoze prisons and jails tomorrow, but as long as they continue to be advanced as the solution, all of the inequalities displaced to crime and punishment will persist. We're in a long game."

Decarceration means getting people out of prisons and jails. Abolitionist and attorney MiAngel Cody helps decarcerate people in federal prison with life sentences for drug-related crime. "I am not a reformist! I'm not an advocate of the reform movement!" Cody told me from her law firm in Chicago. "If this were 1820, we would not be talking about slavery reform. Frederick Douglass and Harriet Tubman were not reformists. Abolition is not a new concept in responding to oppression." To decarcerate people on a national scale, Cody said, her female-led law firm works with high-profile advocates such as Kim Kardashian. "The court of public opinion animates the law," Cody explained. "Courts do not work in an echo chamber. Prosecutors have been manipulating the public opinion for years, and their propaganda machine is extremely effective. They have people thinking you need prisons to feel safe. 'If you do a crime you have to do the time.' It's deeply engrained into the American consciousness."

Many abolitionists argue we need to reconsider how we define crime itself. "I, like many abolitionists, came to abolition because we were tired of harm and we wanted to see something else happening in our communities and in the world. We didn't come idealistically thinking that there was no such thing as harm. Rather, we looked at the political category of crime and wanted to take it apart," said Ruth Wilson Gilmore to the online newspaper *The Intercept*.

When we can view an action as a set of circumstances, rather than a crime with a corresponding number of prison years, the action can be addressed in a more humane, effective way. "Decriminalizing mental-health episodes, fighting homelessness, or decriminalizing drug use are three clear ways to keep people from getting pipelined towards prison. And for abolitionists, we don't just stop at decriminalization: Adequately funding mental-health treatment, providing housing for those in need, and offering adequate rehabilitation services for people with substance dependence are all critical," writes John Washington in his piece for *The Nation*. Many abolitionists believe that not enough is being done to discover and address the root causes of poverty, homelessness, suffering, and addiction.

In many circumstances, punishing people with steep fines and jail and prison time is not the answer. This is causing further harm to individuals and communities. "Criminalizing addiction through drug laws; criminalizing homelessness by conducting sweeps of people sleeping in parks; and criminalizing mental illness by turning prisons into de facto psychiatric hospitals is all treating the symptom instead of the disease," adds Washington. "This is one of the key differences between reform and abolitionism: The former deals with pain management and the latter with the actual source of the pain."

There will probably always be people who will harm themselves or others. The group Christians for the Abolition of Prisons addresses this. Sometimes force must be used when someone is trying to harm another, but we must "continue to respect the dignity of even the most 'predatory' person." The focus must remain on prevention, engaging with people before they commit violence, "not disposing of them by banishing them to some form of detention and ignoring them." Restraint should be implemented by the community, the group says, not the government.

There are ways to prevent violence or stop it from continuing, such as establishing programs and resources in areas considered "million dollar blocks." When someone is released from prison or jail, there are often few opportunities for them, which can result in their returning to jail or prison. Instead, there could be more transitional housing, job opportunities, education, mental healthcare, and addiction counseling readily available in communities, so that when people get out they stay out. Also, preventive programs—like Pat Russo's boxing gym—could open on specific blocks. The focus could shift from punishment to rehabilitation and healing; to prevention, rather than reaction.

Many abolitionists see the billions of dollars being poured into New York City's Borough-Based Jails program as a missed opportunity. Critical Resistance's national communications director, Woods Ervin, said this money would be better spent on decarceration initiatives and in local communities. "The funds that were rapidly located to begin the Borough-Based Jails program could be rerouted to address the needs of those at Rikers and the communities they come from more broadly. . . . 'More humane' jails do not solve the issue of incarceration in this country," Ervin said. "When there are attempts to make punishment more efficient or more friendly, the result is that the power, capacity, and reach of punishment grows, crowding out other opportunities for what could be done to resolve systemic harm in communities."

In 2016, after the death of Kalief Browder, it was in fact an abolition movement that launched calls to close Rikers Island forever. The #CLOSErikers campaign, launched by nonprofit JustLeadershipUSA (JLUSA), demanded Rikers close and the city divest from punishment altogether. I heard it was an uphill battle from the start.

"When I helped launch the campaign to close Rikers Island in 2016, most people in politics were deeply skeptical, if not outright opposed," recalled Janos Marton, who at the time was serving as the director of policy and campaigns for JLUSA. "But along the way, we built a 180-organization coalition, won over nearly every elected official in New York City, forced a commitment to closure from Mayor de Blasio, and watched the city council dramatically pass legislation with a timeline for closure." This abolitionist campaign had championed the Rikers closure and was on track to succeed. The Lippman Commission ran concurrently with the #CLOSErikers campaign. Even though the founder of JLUSA, Glenn Martin, sat on the commission, it seems the message ultimately was co-opted.

"We had a seat at the table, but were distinct from it," Marton recalled. JLUSA argued that Rikers should be closed, without building the new Borough-Based Jails. "But those of us who supported that view didn't do enough to explain how that would work. Members on the 2019 council were largely uninterested in listening. . . . He [Lippman] had progressive ideas, but they weren't as bold. It became a numbers game. 'Should we pass a certain set of reforms?' . . . You create a commission to get to some version of what you want, but with political heft behind it."

A version was, indeed, created. The original message of the #CLOSErikers campaign, however, had changed. Rikers Island would close, but four expensive new jails would be built in the boroughs. According to the Lippman report, "The result is a vision of a twenty-first century criminal justice system that all New Yorkers can be proud of."

Many were not proud. Some were vehemently against the new jails, while other abolitionists accepted this fate, believing that the new jails would at least have fewer beds than the current system. "I'm an abolitionist, but closing Rikers will require—in this current landscape—these Borough-Based Jails. . . . We can't just go zero to sixty," a campaign coordinator at Just Leadership, Brandon Holmes, explained. "It's a strategic way to strip power. . . . Reducing beds and capacity will force prosecutors and police to realize there's not enough room." Holmes believed that moving incarcerated people into communities, instead of isolating them on the island, was a good step. "Here, architecture is important. . . . We need to see a complete transformation of living and working conditions, community and advocacy access. Structural oppression is, literally, right down to the structures and how they exist and operate. . . . As we continue to make these reforms, the Borough-Based facilities is a step. It won't smell like garbage and death." Some of these abolitionists hoped the new Borough-Based Jails could ultimately be repurposed for some other use, outside of the corrections system.

Other abolitionists believe new jails won't fix anything: the Borough-Based Jails program is a cosmetic solution to deep-rooted, structural problems. After Mayor de Blasio announced the Borough-Based Jails program, a group called No New Jails NYC formed in September 2018. They advocate for "the immediate and expedient closure of Rikers without building new jails in any borough in New York City. . . . Instead of committing NYC to a future of incarceration, we can invest billions into our communities and close every jail on Rikers—without opening new jail complexes anywhere in NYC." No New Jails NYC is part of a network that supports a moratorium on all jail construction across the United States, particularly in California via their chapters in San Francisco and Los Angeles. A cage is a cage, they believe, and cannot be reformed. New jails will not solve America's mass-incarceration problem, as Mayor de Blasio had promised. It simply was reinvesting money in the incarceration model. The billions of dollars allocated for new jails should instead be directed to community-based resources to support permanent decarceration.

The #CLOSErikers movement founder, Glenn Martin, is also unconvinced that new jail design will make a difference.

"That comes from people who have never experienced the deprivation of liberty," Martin told me. "You can't convince me design makes a difference. Yes, it's better to be clean. The value is not to make it prettier. In my opinion, the #CLOSErikers campaign lost its way." He paused. "As a formerly incarcerated person, I was in the middle of a liberal reform space, but their rhetoric didn't match my experiences inside. . . . They haven't seen behind the curtain. I have."

"I think it's a mistake," the architect Raphael Sperry told me. "It's a wasted opportunity. It's wasted money they're going to regret."

=====

Three years after Mayor de Blasio announced Rikers would close, the American Institute of Architects' New York chapter made an unprecedented announcement. The group urged architects not to design "unjust, cruel, or harmful spaces of incarceration within the current United States justice system."

"For too long, architects have been complicit in upholding intrinsic racism within the American criminal justice system," the AIA's largest and oldest chapter said in its September 2020 statement. "As architects, we must take on difficult conversations within our workplaces about the broader social implications of our work, and the practices we allow our work to perpetuate."

"We see this as a beginning of a long process. It's a call for action for our members," AIA New York board president Kim Yao told me. "In our code of ethics, it says we will do no harm. These spaces are used for harm and with racial bias. We're one piece of that bigger puzzle, but we felt it was really important to make this statement. . . . We make the buildings that support the system that is fundamentally broken. We want to draw attention to this."

I asked Yao about New York City's Borough-Based Jails program.

"We don't want to be called on to 'pretty up' these spaces," Yao explained. "It's not about making these buildings nicer in the neighborhoods. The system is broken. At a certain point we can't contribute our expertise in a way where the spaces are not being used to rehabilitate. . . . We want to design to solve problems. That's why we love architecture. It takes a lot to say that we shouldn't design these spaces right now. We hope that if our sister chapters take similar stances, we can have better discussions about reshaping what the system is like in the United States."

Raphael Sperry was overjoyed with the NY chapter's stance. "It's fantastic!" he told me. "The problem of racism is that it's widely distributed. Everyone is involved. . . . AIA NY is doing their part and they're calling other people to do their part."

With any major stance comes criticism and controversy. Many were furious in the justice architecture community. "There were varying degrees of outrage," said justice architect Frank Greene, a founding member of the New York chapter of the Academy of Architecture for Justice. "These new facilities are full of light and air and programs and agency, that are not cruel by any definition. Why are these pejorative terms being used?" There was still an opportunity, some felt, to use the Borough-Based Jails program as a force for good; it could still be an international model for how to transform outdated facilities. Greene added, "They should be using this as a template."

What then happened several months later was a watershed moment in the architectural community. This time, it was on a national scale. The American Institute of Architects took a decisive, ethical stance and banned its members from "knowingly designing spaces intended for execution and torture, including indefinite or prolonged solitary confinement of incarcerated people." The AIA had finally changed its tune. "We are committed to promoting the design of a more equitable and just built world that dismantles racial injustice and upholds human rights," the AIA's president, Jane Frederick, said in a statement. "Specifically, AIA members are required to uphold the health, safety and welfare of the public. Spaces for execution, torture and prolonged solitary confinement contradict those values. This decision emphasizes AIA's commitment to making a difference on this issue and upholding human rights for our society."

It was a pivotal moment. Finally, the AIA had changed its code of ethics. Its decision has potential to help change the future of America's jails.

═══

The last time Moose called me from The Boat, he promised he'd be in touch in a couple weeks. A month went by, then another, and another. Concerned, I checked the New York City Department of Correction's online Inmate Lookup Service, which gives a real-time location for anyone currently counted within the city's jail system. I typed in Moose's full name and hit Enter. Three words appeared:

"NO RECORDS FOUND."

There was little recourse to track down Moose. There was

no number to call, no transition housing, no reentry program. I tried his lawyer, friends, and volunteers who knew him through the Rikers Debate Project. Notably, one thing they agreed on was that incarcerating Moose was a huge waste, both for the taxpayers of New York and for Moose himself. Every time Moose called me, his insights left a mark. I always liked hearing what he had to say. He brightened my day, he made me laugh, and he educated me. But when he spoke about his experiences in jail, it was almost as though he felt he belonged in there, spearheading the debates, leading the pack. Maybe on the outside he was distracted, now focused on survival. Or maybe he was seen as a nobody, an "ex-con."

I waited for his call, and I wondered where he was, how he was doing, where he'd slept last night, if he'd managed to find a job. Moose was right: what we need is more programs. But we need more on the outside. It seemed he had been released from the justice system only to be swallowed up by the Free World. He knew his environment greatly affected him. "My opinions are like water," he'd once said. "They take the shape of the place I'm in." Inside, he'd been so eager to share his story, but outside, he'd become a ghost. I waited, but he didn't call.

TEN

The Future

When I began reporting on the Borough-Based Jails program, there seemed to be many conflicting opinions on how to move forward with justice. One by one I listened to incarcerated people, formerly incarcerated people, abolitionists, jail and prison volunteers, family members, law enforcement officers, neighbors, and architects. I soon realized that many voices were actually singing in harmony. It just required a more attuned ear.

Incarceration doesn't work as crime prevention, they said. If it did, the United States would be one of the safest countries in the world. Building the next generation to be safer, healthier, and more equitable will require a shift in how we view justice. Repeatedly, many people told me the priorities are upside down. We need to be investing in effective prevention, community programs, education, and restorative justice. Building new jails is not the answer, they said. The solutions live outside these walls.

"I think that we need to get away from thinking about the justice system as the way in which we secure our safety," said none other than the former director of New York City's Mayor's Office of Criminal Justice Liz Glazer, in a video on a prison abolition group's website. After Glazer resigned from her bureaucratic post, she joined the Square One Project, an abolition nonprofit dedicated to "imagining a future for justice and public safety that starts from scratch—from square one—instead of tinkering at the edges or cherry-picking cordoned-off areas for reform." It seemed she was finally giving the answer to my "curveball question" I'd asked her at 1 Centre Street. In another turn of events, the former bureaucrat also launched her own nonprofit, Vital City, which promotes public safety through housing, jobs, decent schools, and active public spaces. It seemed Glazer was no longer invested in new jails, instead devoting her time to initiatives outside the justice system she once helped steer.

Other officials, too, were creating more programs to improve quality of life and decrease arrests. Though Cops & Kids couldn't raise money or receive grants from the government, Pat Russo and his team of law-enforcement volunteers raised enough private donations to open another Cops & Kids boxing gym. Larger than the Park Hill space, this 3,000-square-foot gym opened in Flatbush Gardens, Brooklyn. When I visited in the spring of 2022, it was fully loaded with new equipment, a built-in tutoring and career-path center, and local kids exhilarated about boxing. "The answer is: give these kids a positive alternative to gangs and streets and drug sales and stuff and save them, which is crime prevention," Russo said. "I've been doing this thirty years. The common denominator is every kid that moved on from the program, they'll tell you, if it wasn't for being around positive people and having a positive place to go every day to occupy their time, they'd be dead or in jail. It's crime prevention." I asked the retired cop if he felt there were enough prevention programs in New York City. "Without a doubt you need to have more," Russo responded. "The kids we deal with are hard, they're hard to deal with"—Russo dabbed tears from his eyes—"they're troubled, very difficult, they come with a lot of baggage. . . . They have nothing at home." The boxing program was making a difference, one child at a time.

Camilla Broderick, too, was doing her part. While she was still branded a felon, Broderick found a job at a New York City nonprofit, where her actions help people in need and potentially prevent arrests. Every day of the workweek, Broderick walks her territory—the crowded streets of Times Square—where she seeks out people struggling with drugs or who are in need of a place to sleep or eat. With their permission, she helps them find food, shelter, or a safe place to sober up. Informed by her own experiences, Broderick hopes to deter as many people as possible from jail time by helping them connect to the resources they need.

People are taking small but mighty steps to build a more equitable society within their own areas of influence. They are becoming more accountable, speaking up for what they believe in, and taking action. All these individual and organizational actions are contributing to a change in perspective on what constitutes "justice." When we ask our neighbor how she's doing, or if we can help watch her children while she's at work, that is prison abolition. When we ask a distressed stranger how we can help, we are engaged in abolition. When we stand up for someone who's being mistreated, that is abolition. It's the little steps we take as individuals in our communities that make our communities safer. Investing in safe housing, free children's programs, and quality education is police reform. When we work outside the criminal justice system to help stop violence before it even begins, that is abolition.

There are many people and organizations working outside the criminal justice system to prevent crime, promote healing, and build safer communities. At this point, many efforts are grassroots, rather than institutional. These resources and programs need to be connected in a way that's accessible. As history shows, where there is political will, funding and resources follow. A whole economy and infrastructure were created to support mass incarceration. Can a new infrastructure be designed to prevent harm and violence, and to stop it from happening again? Where there's demand, money flows.

While we can begin to shift away from our current definitions of justice, we can also help prepare people currently in jails and prisons for a life outside, once they are released. Today, when people are released from jails and prisons, the Free World often offers few opportunities and places to turn. As America's high recidivism rate shows, it's only a matter of time before many are locked back up again. Reentry needs to be prioritized and better funded, my sources told me. Reentry is a huge focus elsewhere: countries like Sweden and Norway position prisons as places of rehabilitation, where correction officers are trained to help prepare incarcerated people for success once released. In America, little help is offered for making the transition.

Greg Cook is offering his help. Since his early days at HOK, his career as a justice architect has evolved. When Cook abandoned the corporate corrections market in 2021, he took steps in his own community to design spaces he believes in. At a regional architecture firm in Washington State, he designs buildings for rehabilitation and reentry. This is a way he believes he can use the built environment to better his community. This new position "is allowing me to focus on the most rewarding part of the work I've done, which has been focused on treatment and rehabilitation and supporting people as they return to their communities," Cook told me. Unlike his work at HOK and HDR, which required extensive travel in the United States and abroad, Cook's current role allows him to design facilities in the area where he lives, which he said sends an important message. "I'm invested and committed to the long-term success of the programs we are implementing and supporting," he explained. "To me, focusing on that aspect of it has kept me engaged and enthusiastic about how architecture can support a rehabilitative and restorative approach to justice and the overall health of our communities." This philosophy of focusing on successful reentry could lower America's high recidivism rate, so that when incarcerated people are let out, they stay out.

While Cook dedicates his architectural prowess to reentry and rehabilitation spaces, other architects are designing restorative-justice programs, education centers, and work programs. Designing Justice + Designing Spaces is an example of a nonprofit architecture and real estate development firm that works to "counter the societal inequities evident in the dominant architectural models of courthouses and prisons." "You can't reform a system built on racism . . . you're always going to be putting lipstick on the pig," the group's cofounder, Deanna Van Buren told me.

Fifty years ago, the federal government attempted to reform the justice system. The Department of Justice turned to architects to learn how it could improve prisons and jails. A qualified team of architects, social scientists, correctional administrators, and psychologists* observed 100 prisons and jails across America. Their research was published in 1973 as *The New Red Barn: A Critical Look at the Modern Prison*. What it advised was likely far different from what the DOJ expected.

"The local jail is the most inexcusable part of our entire criminal justice system. It is a garbage can. It receives that residue for which society has provided no intelligent solutions," wrote *New Red Barn* author William Nagel. The report warned the government of the peril and overall ineffectiveness of prisons and jails. "These facilities do not reduce harm and render society safer; they inflict further harm and often leave those inside worse than from when they came in." Speaking in language similar to abolitionists, Nagel said the answers would be found in social improvement, not inside "physical plants in which imprisonment takes place."

"The correctional monuments that this generation should bequeath to the next should not be Bentham's Panopticon, Haviland's Cherry Hill [Eastern State Penitentiary], HOK's Marion, Curtis and Davis's Fox Lake, or even Gruzen's Leesburg. It should be a series of improvements in our society and our criminal justice processes which, in their combined effect, reduce

---

* The nonprofit organization in charge of the study, the American Foundation's Institute of Corrections, assembled the team and handled the costs associated with the study and field research.

markedly the use of imprisonment in our land," he wrote. The United States "must replace a penal system which has proved not only inhumane, but nonproductive."

These critical insights had potential to change history. But evidently, the government didn't heed the advice it sought. After *The New Red Barn* was published, America's incarcerated population ballooned 700 percent. The nation experienced the largest construction boom of prisons and jails in history. Now, we stand on the brink of the next generation.

If we can build jails and prisons en masse, then we can build restorative-justice facilities, transitional housing, and reentry centers en masse. Can we have as many restorative-justice centers as we've had correctional facilities? Can we have more colleges and universities than prisons and jails? If there were a plethora of effective programs and buildings available, could we eventually place a moratorium on new construction of prisons and jails? Many of the nation's prisons and jails could one day be deemed outdated and unnecessary, their architecture and philosophies passé, making way for a new generation of justice architecture to take hold.

In February 2023, nearly 6,000 people were incarcerated at Rikers. The previous year, more people had died on Rikers than in the last quarter of a century. Rikers seemed worse than ever. Long delays in the legal system extend untried people's stays in jail. Some city officials expect the situation to get worse. New York City correction commissioner Louis Molina said the city's jail population will likely grow to 7,000 by the end of the year.

Mayor Eric Adams agreed, adding that the Borough-Based Jails program needs to be reevaluated.

"Kudos to Molina for being honest and candid—that we need to look at this plan and we need a Plan B," Mayor Adams told the website *The City*. "And, because this [the BBJ program] is costing us close to $10 billion, we can have a better use of our tax dollars and I stand with him and I agree with him. And I think the City Council must reassess this plan." The question still lingers of how the city will proceed. It already started to dismantle the Tombs and the Brooklyn Detention Complex. Construction at the Queens site has begun. Some fear New York City will build four new jails in the boroughs but keep Rikers Island.

Then, Mayor Adams said something that was perhaps most revealing of all. "You have to work really hard to go to Rikers," Adams told *The City*, "for the most part, being placed in Rikers means that you are a bad person that you did something probably extremely violent."

With this brand of political rhetoric, it seems we've reverted to the era of mass incarceration. New York City's mayor was using the same old messaging and fearmongering politicians have used for centuries. However, it is awareness of the criminal justice system and how it operates that allows us to confront misleading statements and understand why the justice system was created, who's incarcerated there, and why it's not working. Only when we understand our stereotypes, myths, and failures can we change our notions of justice and find effective ways to better society.

To be a beacon of hope and aspiration—as E. B. White called New York City in *Here Is New York*—the citizen's needs have to be met, and we have to use successful approaches to deal with violence and harm. We can build a society where every child has opportunity for free programs, a good education, and mentorship; where people have access to mental-health services and affordable housing; where people aren't penalized for using drugs or for not having enough cash to afford bail. Even for violent offenders, there could be other forms of effective recourse to prevent violence from happening again. Interconnected services can be created, with investment in high-risk communities, education, health services, transitioning programs, jobs, and crime prevention.

If New York City can invest in communities, reentry, and programs outside the justice system, other jurisdictions can follow. We can avoid having so many people caged in the nation's jails—many of them untried—costing taxpayers billions of dollars, and their cycling through the system over and over again. If our political leaders continue to deem scores of untried incarcerated folks "bad people," and if we continue to put our money and ideas of justice into incarceration, then we will stay in this endless loop. As the cop and boxer Joel cautioned at the Park Hill gym, if jails are built, they will be filled.

———

Since Moose was released, two years had passed. I'd heard no word from him. I wondered if he was still alive.

Until one wintry afternoon in 2023, when my phone rang.

As I answered, an automated voice said I had a call from the New York City Department of Correction.

"What's up, Eva? Long time!" the familiar, upbeat voice crackled through the line. In the background was clanking and shouting, the unforgettable sounds of Rikers Island.

Acknowledgments

Thank you to my husband, Benjamin Massey, for your uncon-
ditional love, insights, and encouragement. Mom, your endless
support and readings have been critical through this process, and
I appreciate you so much. Dad, you encourage me to question, to
be bold, and to be fearless, which helped shape the woman I am
today. G & G, Sis, Masenne, Atlas, and Alex, thank you for your
love and your individual wisdom.

To my agent at Janklow & Nesbit, Ian Bonaparte, you have believed in me and this book from the beginning; thank you for standing behind me and for your continued care and friendship. Hannah
Murphy Winter, your guidance is invaluabale. Thank you to Avid
Reader and Simon & Schuster for making this book possible.

To my friends, family, and colleagues who provided crucial readings, support, and advice over these years: Jake Goodman, Kate Edgar, Emma Jenney, Ifrah Ahmed, Jackie Massey
Clark, Jerry Goldman, Laura Michel, Dillon Storey, Nick Mafi,
Caroline Blacque, jackie sumell, Khiteriara Brown, Rich Wener,
Adam Robb, Martin Stigsgaard, Steve Nishimoto, Caitlin Hal-
pern, and the Rikers Debate Club. Each of you provided unique
support and I am grateful for you.

I have much gratitude for every one of you who chose to
share your stories with me. I deeply appreciate my sources, without whom *These Walls* would not have been possible.

Notes

ONE: Rikers Island

1 **None was more dysfunctional:** Mayor's Office of Criminal Justice, "Safely Reducing New York City's Jail Population," NYC.gov (website), report, accessed March 10, 2023, https://web.archive.org/web/20170408161451/https://www.nyc.gov/site/criminaljustice/work/jail-population.page.

2 **Situated between the boroughs:** Jonathan Lippman et al., *A More Just New York City: Independent Commission on New York City Criminal Justice and Incarceration Reform*, commission report, April 2017, https://static1.squarespace.com/static/5b6de4731aef1de914f43628/t/5b96c6f81ae6cf5e9c5f186d/1536607993842/Lippman%2BCommission%2BReport%2BFINAL%2BSingles.pdf.

2 **The city annually spends:** Lippman et al., *More Just New York City*, 2017, p. 14.

2 **It was like sitting:** Various incarcerated people, interviewed by author, at various New York City jails throughout 2020.

3 **New York City's total jail population:** Criminal Justice Agency, "New York City Jail Population Reduction in the time of COVID-19," City of New York (website), report, April 30, 2020, page 1, https://criminaljustice.cityofnewyork.us/wp-content/uploads/2020/05/COVID-factsheet_APRIL-30-2020.pdf.

7 **For those in jail:** Lippman et al., *More Just New York City*, 2017.

7 **The average bail runs:** Wendy Sawyer and Peter Wagner, "Mass Incarceration: The Whole Pie 2022," Prison Policy Initiative (website), fact sheet, March 14, 2022, https://www.prisonpolicy .org/reports/pie2022.html.

7 **A survey found:** Michael Rempel and Zachary Katznelson, *Halfway to History: Five-Year Status Report on the Path to Closing Rikers*, A More Just NYC (website), report, October 2022, p. 2, https://static1.squarespace.com/static/5b6de4731aef1de914f436 28/t/635aca855d4769714639828a/1666894470433/Half way+to+History+-+Five+Year+Status+Report+re+Closing +RIkers.pdf.

7 **Those who received mental:** Rempel and Katznelson, *Halfway to History*, p. 2.

7 **In New York City's jails:** Lippman et al., *More Just New York City*, 2017, p. 13.

8 **Nationally, Black people are:** The Sentencing Project (website), report, April 19, 2018, https://www.sentencingproject .org/reports/report-to-the-united-nations-on-racial-dispari ties-in-the-u-s-criminal-justice-system/#footnote-ref-4.

8 **The city comptroller reported:** New York City (website), "Comptroller Stringer: Cost of Incarceration per Person in New York City Skyrockets to All-Time High," press release, December 6, 2021, https://comptroller.nyc.gov/newsroom /comptroller-stringer-cost-of-incarceration-per-person-in -new-york-city-skyrockets-to-all-time-high-2/.

8 **Jails see over 10:** Sawyer and Wagner, "Mass Incarceration."

8 **The United States has:** Sawyer and Wagner, "Mass Incarceration."

8 **Of all the people:** Luke Scrivner et al., "New York City Jail

Population in 2019," Data Collaborative for Justice, report, 2020, https://datacollaborativeforjustice.org/work/jail/new -york-city-jail-population-in-2019/.

8 **There are 1,566 state prisons:** Leah Wang et al., "Beyond the Count: A Deep Dive into State Prison Populations," Prison Policy Initiative (website), April 2022, https://www.prisonpolicy.org /reports/beyondthecount.html.

8 **Those who break:** Federal Bureau of Prisons (website), "About Our Facilities," accessed June 7, 2022, https://www.bop.gov/about /facilities/federal_prisons.jsp.

8 **Private prisons, run by:** Sawyer and Wagner, "Mass Incarceration."

9 **We have more:** Course description of Advanced Design Studio, Frank O. Gehry and Trattie Davies, 2017, https://www.architec ture.yale.edu/courses/13736-frank-gehry.

9 **With 3,116 local jails:** Sawyer and Wagner, "Mass Incarceration."

9 **"I hate having to give this":** Joel Huffer, phone interview with author, June 14, 2021.

9 **Our recidivism rate is:** Matthew R. Durose and Leonardo Antenangeli, "Recidivism of Prisoners Released in 34 States in 2012: A 5-year Follow-Up Period," Bureau of Justice Statistics (website), July 2021, https://bjs.ojp.gov/library/publications /recidivism-prisoners-released-34-states-2012-5-year-follow -period-2012-2017.

10 **Of all the arrests:** Vera Institute of Justice (website), "What Policing Costs: A Look at Spending in America's Biggest Cities," June 26, 2020, https://www.vera.org/publications/what-polic ing-costs-in-americas-biggest-cities.

10 **In the words of historian:** Arthur M. Schlesinger Jr., *The Cycles of American History* (Boston: Houghton Mifflin, 1986), p. xviii.

11   **In 1664:** Michelle O'Donnell, "Farmhouse Called Home Is a Home to History, Too," *New York Times*, October 11, 2016, https://www.nytimes.com/2006/10/11/nyregion/11farmhouse.html.

11   **The rancid smells:** Chelsia Rose Marcius, " 'Filthy Mess': How Robert Moses Tried to Deal with Rikers' Methane Gas Problem," *Daily News*, December 23, 2019, https://www.nydailynews.com/new-york/ny-rikers-island-history-environment-methane-gas-20191223-aalt4qjqcvbc5gvwag6sjhmorm-story.html.

12   **Twice, the city attempted:** Insha Rahman, "Closing Rikers Island: In Support of a Yes Vote on October 17," Vera Institute of Justice (website), October 8, 2019, https://www.vera.org/blog/closing-rikers-island.

13   **In 2015, the city:** Benjamin Weiser, "New York City Settles Suit Over Abuses at Rikers Island," *New York Times*, June 22, 2015, https://www.nytimes.com/2015/06/23/nyregion/new-york-city-settles-suit-over-abuses-at-rikers-island.html.

13   **As of March 2023:** New York State Department of Corrections and Community Services, "DOCCS COVID-19 Report," February 21, 2023, https://doccs.ny.gov/doccs-covid-19-report.

13   **Nearly all criminal cases:** Lippman et al., *More Just New York City*, 2017, p. 57.

14   **Browder spent more than 700:** Jennifer Gonnerman, "Before the Law," *New Yorker,* September 29, 2014, https://www.newyorker.com/magazine/2014/10/06/before-the-law.

15   **"Kalief entered as a child":** "Speaker Mark-Viverito's 2016 State of the City Address, Remarks as Prepared for Delivery," New York City Council (website), press release, February 11, 2016, https://council.nyc.gov/press/2016/02/11/46/; NYC Council (@NYCCouncil), "Speaker Melissa Mark-Viverito delivers 2016 #StateofNYC address," February 16, 2016, YouTube

video, 1:33:34, https://www.youtube.com/watch?v=H_DuVZ
PiAyM.

16 **Then New York governor:** Colby Hamilton, "Cuomo Offers
Support for Mark-Viverito's Call to Close Rikers," *Politico*, February 14, 2016, https://www.politico.com/states/new-york
/albany/story/2016/02/cuomo-offers-support-for-mark-viver
itos-call-to-close-rikers-031267.

16 **In early 2016:** David J. Goodman, "De Blasio Says Idea of
Closing Rikers Jail Complex Is Unrealistic," *New York Times*,
February 16, 2016, https://www.nytimes.com/2016/02/17/ny
region/de-blasio-says-idea-of-closing-rikers-jail-complex-is-un
realistic.html.

16 **more philanthropic dollars:** Funders Summit on Justice Reform, "The Nation's Eyes on Rikers: A Report on Community
Leader-Identified Priorities, Opportunities for Funders and Key
Organizing Objective," report, Philanthropy New York (website), June 2018, https://philanthropynewyork.org/resources
/nation-s-eyes-rikers-report-community-leader-identified-pri
orities-opportunities-funders.

17 **"New York City":** New York City (website), "Mayor de Blasio,
Speaker Mark-Viverito Announce 10 Year Plan to Close Rikers Island," transcript, March 31, 2017, https://www.nyc.gov
/office-of-the-mayor/news/196-17/transcript-mayor-de-bla
sio-speaker-mark-viverito-10-year-plan-close-rikers-island;
Associated Press (@AssociatedPress), "NYC Mayor Wants
Rikers Island Closed in Decade," March 31, 2017, YouTube
video, 1:02, https://www.youtube.com/watch?v=F5Z1m2m
bLaY.

18 **In 2017, the average:** New York City (website), "Mayor de Blasio Announces 'Smaller, Safer, Fairer: A Roadmap to Closing
Rikers Island,'" press release, June 22, 2017, https://www.nyc

.gov/office-of-the-mayor/news/427-17/mayor-de-blasio-small
er-safer-fairer--roadmap-closing-rikers-island-.

19   **The new façades could:** Lippman et al., *A More Just New York City*, 2017, p. 79.

19   **"[Rikers] is the epitome":** Judge Jonathan Lippman, phone interview with author, July 9, 2020.

20   **In the early days:** New York City, "Mayor de Blasio Announces 'Smaller, Safer.'"

20   **New York City has paved:** Martha Biondi, "How New York Changes the Story of the Civil Rights Movement," NYC.gov (website), report, accessed March 7, 2023, https://www.nyc .gov/html/cchr/justice/downloads/pdf/how_new_york _changes_the_civil_rights_movement.pdf.

20   **During the last 20 years:** Lippman et al., *A More Just New York City*, 2017, p. 23.

21   **Borough-Based Jails program:** Rempel and Katznelson, *Half-way to History.*

21   **later pushed to August 31:** JB Nicholas, "Plan to Close Rikers and Build New Jails Faces Significant Delays," *Gothamist*, August 12, 2020, https://gothamist.com/news/plan-close-rikers -and-build-new-jails-faces-significant-delays.

21   **To ensure successful execution:** Implementation Task Force, "Closing Rikers: Ensuring Effective Implementation," City of New York (website), news report, accessed March 18, 2022, https://rikers.cityofnewyork.us/implementation-task-force/.

21   **The Lippman Commission and the City:** Reuven Blau, Haidee Chu, and Stephon Johnson, "City Hall Still Planning for Shutdown of Rikers Island Jails, But Is Mayor All-In?" *The City*, December 29, 2022, https://www.thecity .nyc/2022/12/29/23529990/does-nyc-mayor-adams-sup port-rikers-shutdown.

21 **Rikers Island was mandated:** Jonah E. Bromwich and Nicholas Fandos, "Eric Adams Says He Wants to Close Rikers, It May Not Be That Simple," *New York Times*, December 17, 2021, https://www.nytimes.com/2021/12/17/nyregion/eric-adams-rikers-island.html.

TWO: Imprisonment

26 **Until this point, imprisonment:** Michael Ignatieff, *A Just Measure of Pain: The Penitentiary in the Industrial Revolution 1750–1850* (London: Pantheon Books, 1978), p. 15.

26 **"The public execution":** Michel Foucault, *Discipline and Punish: The Birth of the Prison* (New York: Pantheon, 1977), p. 49.

26 **"Till the end of the eighteenth":** Arthur M. Schlesinger Jr., *The Cycles of American History* (Boston: Houghton Mifflin, 1986), p. 88.

27 **"The panoptic mechanism":** Foucault, *Discipline and Punish*, p. 200.

28 **"Jailers were not salaried":** BBC, Historic Figures, John Howard (1726–1790), accessed February 3, 2023, https://www.bbc.co.uk/history/historic_figures/howard_john.shtml.

28 **In America, much:** Friends Committee on National Legislation (website), "Quakers Know Prison from the Inside Out," September 29, 2016, https://www.fcnl.org/updates/2016-09/quakers-know-prisons-inside-out.

29 **The state of Pennsylvania:** William G. Nagel, *The New Red Barn: A Critical Look at the Modern American Prison* (New York: Walker, 1973), p. 8.

29 **The state launched:** Nagel, *New Red Barn*, p. 8.

29 **Haviland won:** Richard E. Wener, *The Environmental Psychology of Prisons and Jails: Creating Humane Spaces in Secure Settings* (Cambridge: Cambridge University Press, 2012), p. 24.

30 **Inside, each incarcerated person:** Nagel, *New Red Barn*, p. 92.

30 **"In the Pennsylvanian":** Foucault, *Discipline and Punish*, p. 239.

30 **Haviland's structure:** Wener, *Environmental Psychology of Prisons and Jails*, p. 28.

32 **"You're standing inside":** Steve Buscemi, *Eastern State Penitentiary Historic Site Audio Tour Script*, Eastern State Penitentiary Historic Site (website), updated May 2019, https://www.easternstate.org/explore/audio-tour.

33 **Eastern was, in fact:** Nagel, *New Red Barn*, p. 9.

33 **it had plumbing:** Chai Woodham, "Eastern State Penitentiary: A Prison With a Past," *Smithsonian*, September 30, 2008, https://www.smithsonianmag.com/history/eastern-state-penitentiary-a-prison-with-a-past-14274660/.

33 **What could be:** Vera Institute of Justice (website), "Reimagining Prison: Design Strategies to Increase Public Safety and Improve Societal Well-Being," October 2018, https://www.vera.org/publications/reimagining-prison-print-report.

33 **Solitary confinement quickly:** Nagel, *New Red Barn*, p. 8.

33 **"within a short space":** Foucault, *Discipline and Punish*, p. 116.

34 **Imprisonment was adopted:** Eastern State Penitentiary (website), "Timeline," accessed July 9, 2021, https://www.easternstate.org/research/history-eastern-state/timeline.

35 **"not one redeeming principle":** As quoted in Buscemi, *Site Audio Tour Script*.

35 **Meanwhile, in New York:** Vera Institute of Justice, "Reimagining Prison."

36 **At Sing Sing:** Sing Sing Prison Museum (website), "About Sing Sing Prison: History," accessed March 4, 2022, http://www.singsingprisonmuseum.org/history-of-sing-sing-prison.html.

36 **Many of Sing Sing's cells:** Wener, *Environmental Psychology of Prisons and Jails*, p. 31.

36 **Embedded in:** U.S. Constitution, Thirteenth Amendment, https://www.archives.gov/historical-docs/13th-amendment.

36 **This clause allowed for:** Ava DuVernay, director, *13th* (Sherman Oaks, CA: Forward Movement / Kandoo Films, 2016), film.

36 **During this period:** Christopher R. Adamson, "Punishment after Slavery: Southern State Penal Systems, 1865–1890," *Social Problems* 30, no. 5 (1983): 555–569, https://doi.org/10.2307 /800272.

36 **In a perverse twist:** Whitney Benns, "American Slavery, Reinvented," *The Atlantic*, September 21, 2015, https://www .theatlantic.com/business/archive/2015/09/prison-labor-in -america/406177/.

37 **"In 1880, former Confederate":** "USA: The Violent History of Angola Prison," *Prison Insider*, May 4, 2020, https://www .prison-insider.com/en/articles/etats-unis-the-violent-history -of-angola-prison.

37 **To this day:** Benns, "American Slavery, Reinvented."

37 **The first paradigm:** Vera Institute of Justice, "Reimagining Prison."

38 **In 1930, the Federal:** Federal Bureau of Prisons (website), "Alcatraz Origins," https://www.bop.gov/about/history/alcatraz.jsp.

THREE: The Justice Architects

42 **"I never realized":** Gregory Cook, Zoom interview with author, August 5, 2021.

43 **By 2014, when Cook:** American Institute of Architects (website), Academy of Architecture for Justice, national conference program, November 2014, https://network.aia.org/viewdocu ment/2014-aaj-conference-program?CommunityKey=6cb91d7 c-05dc-4b48-97ea-b36b6034093e&tab=librarydocuments.

45 **As of 2021:** Ella Fassler, "A Company That Designs Jails Is Spying on Activists Who Oppose Them," *Vice*, August 17, 2021, https://www.vice.com/en/article/93ym4z/a-company -that-designs-jails-is-spying-on-activists-who-oppose-them.

47 **They reviewed over:** Fred Moyer (head of the National Clearinghouse for Criminal Justice Planning and Architecture), phone interview with author, January 26, 2022.

48 **"The confinement of man":** Task Force on Correctional Architecture, American Institute of Architecture, American Institute of Architects, minutes from meeting sent via email to author, September 6–8, 1972, p. 38.

48 **In the past, many:** Task Force on Correctional Architecture, minutes, p. 12.

48 **The conference aimed to:** Task Force on Correctional Architecture, minutes, ED-5.

49 **By 1975, the:** Task Force on Correctional Architecture, minutes, ED-6.

49 **Today, the AAJ:** Bruce Bland (senior director of AIA Knowledge Communities), email interview and correspondence with author, December 15, 2021.

49 **"it might be the most":** Christopher Hawthorne, "Prison Design Faces Judgement," *Los Angeles Times*, August 30, 2013, https://www.latimes.com/entertainment/arts/la-xpm-2013 -aug-30-la-et-cm-prison-architecture-20130901-story.html.

49 **From the White House:** Nazish Dholakia and Jamila Hodge, "Fifty Years Ago Today, President Nixon Declared the War on Drugs," Vera Institute of Justice (website), June 17, 2021, https://www.vera.org/news/fifty-years-ago-today-president -nixon-declared-the-war-on-drugs.

49 **"There was a whole type":** Frank Greene (chair of the Academy of Architecture for Justice [AAJ] Advisory Group and

founding member of the New York chapter of AAJ), phone interview with author, December 3, 2021.

50 **On February 4, 2020:** NYC Department of Design and Construction, "City Issues Requests for Qualifications for Design and Construction of Four New Borough-Based Jails," NYC .gov (website), press release, February 4, 2020, https://www .prnewswire.com/news-releases/city-issues-request-for-quali fications-for-design-and-construction-of-four-new-borough -based-jails-301005306.html.

51 **Each jail was a massive undertaking:** Roger Lichtman, phone interview with author, June 15, 2022.

51 **Thanks to new legislation:** Construction Dive (website), "Gov. Cuomo signs NYC design-build legislation," January 2, 2020, https://www.constructiondive.com/news/gov -cuomo-signs-nyc-design-build-legislation/569680/#:~:text =Andrew%20Cuomo%20signed%20into%20law,governor %20for%20his%20signature%20Dec.

51 **one single point of contact:** NYC Department of Design and Construction, "City Issues Request for Qualifications."

51 **Design-build teams:** Michael Kimmelman, "After Rikers Island Closes, What Will Jail Look Like?," *New York Times*, December 18, 2019, https://www.nytimes.com/2019/12/18 /arts/design/rikers-island-new-jails.html.

51 **The agency awarded a $107.4 million:** NYC Department of Design and Construction, "NYC Department of Design and Construction Seeks Industry Input on the Development of New York City's Design-Build Borough Based Jails Program," NYC .gov (website), press release, June 13, 2019, https://www.nyc.gov /site/ddc/about/press-releases/2019/DDC-Seeks-Industry-In put-On-BBJ.page.

52 **Together with construction firm:** AECOM (website),

"AECOM-led Joint Venture Awarded Notable Design-Build Program Contract for City of New York," press release, May 29, 2019, https://aecom.com/sa/press-releases/aecom-led-joint-venture-awarded-notable-design-build-program-contract-for-city-of-new-york/.

52 **The Manhattan-based jail:** NYC Department of Design and Construction, *Design Principles and Guidelines for Manhattan Facility*, City of New York (website), January 2022, https://www.nyc.gov/assets/ddc/downloads/DDC-Guiding-Principles-2016.pdf; https://rikers.cityofnewyork.us/documents/manhattan-site-design-principles-guidelines/.

52 **The Brooklyn jail's:** NYC Department of Design and Construction, *Design Principles and Guidelines for Brooklyn Facility*, City of New York (website), January 2022, https://rikers.cityofnewyork.us/wp-content/uploads/BBJ-BK-FAC-Design-Principles-and-Guidelines-Public-Version-220516-1.pdf.

52 **Indirect supervision presupposes:** Dholakia and Hodge, "Fifty Years Ago Today."

52 **The philosophy of direct:** Wener, *Environmental Psychology of Prisons and Jails*, pp. 46–47.

53 **"It is hard for someone":** Wener, *Environmental Psychology of Prisons and Jails*, p. 46.

54 **When the concept of:** Wener, *Environmental Psychology of Prisons and Jails*, p. 47.

54 **There were also:** Wener, *Environmental Psychology of Prisons and Jails*, p. 48.

54 **"Not only were conditions":** Correctional News, "Background Check: The Game Changer," August 10, 2012, https://correctionalnews.com/2012/08/10/background-check-the-game-changer/.

55 **"It really challenged my beliefs":** Gregory Cook, phone interview with author, April 30, 2020.

FOUR: The Incarcerated

57 **This giant barge:** Sewlyn Raab, "Bronx Jail Barge to Open, Though the Cost Is Steep," *New York Times*, January 27, 1992, https://www.nytimes.com/1992/01/27/nyregion/bronx-jail -barge-to-open-though-the-cost-is-steep.html.

58 **Able to hold 800:** Matthew Haag, "A Floating Jail Was Supposed to Be Temporary, That Was 27 Years Ago," *New York Times*, October 10, 2019, https://www.nytimes.com/2019/10/10/nyre gion/nyc-jail-barge-rikers.html.

60 **New York City has:** Graeme Wood, "How Gangs Took Over Prisons," *The Atlantic*, October 2014, https://www.theatlantic .com/magazine/archive/2014/10/how-gangs-took-over-pris ons/379330/.

60 **A 2019 study by:** Lauren Brinkley-Rubeinstein et al., "Association of Restrictive Housing During Incarceration with Mortality After Release," *Journal of the American Medical Association*, October 4, 2019, https://jamanetwork.com/journals/jamanet workopen/fullarticle/2752350.

61 **Rapper Lil Wayne:** Lil Wayne, *Gone 'Til November: A Journal of Rikers Island* (New York: Plume, 2016), p. 139.

62 **Even though Black people:** American Civil Liberties Union, "Mass Incarceation: An Animated Series," https://www.aclu .org/issues/smart-justice/mass-incarceration/mass-incarcera tion-animated-series.

63 **"People tell us":** Stanley Richards, phone interview with author, May 13, 2020.

63 **Michelle Alexander reported:** Michelle Alexander, *The New Jim Crow: Mass Incarceration in the Age of Colorblindness* (New York: New Press, 2012), p. 5.

64 **For instance, while New York City spends:** Emma G. Fitz-simmons, "Mayor's Proposed Cuts to Libraries Will Hurt

New Yorkers, Leaders Say," *New York Times,* January 11, 2023, https://www.nytimes.com/2023/01/11/nyregion/library -funding-cuts-eric-adams.html.

64 **$421 million on:** Greg B. Smith, "The Bronx Hall of Justice Is Falling Apart and No One Knows How to Stop It," The City (website), February 20, 2022, https://www.thecity .nyc/2022/2/20/22942537/bronx-hall-of-justice-falling-apart.

65 **In the first two weeks:** Stanford Executive Sessions on Sentencing and Corrections, "The First 72 Hours of Reentry: Seizing the Moment of Release," Stanford Law School (website), report, September 12, 2008, https://law.stanford.edu/index.php ?webauth-document=child-page/266901/doc/slspublic/Seizing _the_Moment_Release_091208.pdf.

65 **According to a report:** Stanford Executive Sessions, "First 72 Hours."

65 **As Richards said:** Richards, interview.

66 **Many others feel:** Lindsey Davis, "View from the Street: Unsheltered New Yorkers and the Need for Safety, Dignity, and Agency," Coalition for the Homeless (website), survey results, April 2021, https://www.coalitionforthehomeless.org/wp-con tent/uploads/2021/04/View-from-the-Street-April-21.pdf.

66 **In the last 40 years:** New York City Independent Budget Office, "Albany Shifts the Burden: As the Cost for Sheltering the Homeless Rises, Federal and City Funds Are Increasingly Tapped," fiscal brief, October 2015, https://www.ibo.nyc .ny.us/iboreports/albany-shifts-the-burden-as-the-cost-for -sheltering-the-homeless-rises-federal-city-funds-are-increas ingly-tapped-october-2015.pdf.

67 **The majority of people:** Davis, "View from the Street," p. 28.

67 **In New York City:** Mihir Zaveri, "NYC Official Plans to Fill Manhattan's Empty Space," *New York Times*, January 31, 2023,

https://www.nytimes.com/2023/01/31/nyregion/manhattan
-housing-vacant-buildings.html.

67 **Nationwide, housing:** Up for Growth, "New Report: U.S. Fell
7.3 Million Units Behind Housing Demand from 2000–2015,"
news release, April 16, 2018, https://www.globenewswire
.com/en/news-release/2018/04/16/1472315/0/en/New-re
port-U-S-fell-7-3-million-units-behind-housing-demand
-from-2000-2015.html.

67 **On average, they have:** Emily Peiffer, "Five Charts That Explain
the Homelessness-Jail Cycle—and How to Break It," Urban.org
(website), September 16, 2020, https://www.urban.org/features
/five-charts-explain-homelessness-jail-cycle-and-how-break-it.

68 **One report out:** Fei Wu and Max Stevens, "The Services
Homeless Single Adults Use and their Associated Costs: An
Examination of Utilization Patterns and Expenditures in Los
Angeles County over One Fiscal Year," January 2016, https://
homeless.lacounty.gov/wp-content/uploads/2019/02/home
less-costs-final.pdf.

68 **In Connecticut:** Alexi Jones, "New Data: The Revolving Door
Between Homeless Shelters and Prisons in Connecticut," Prison
Policy Initiative (website), blog, February 10, 2021, https://
www.prisonpolicy.org/blog/2021/02/10/homelessness/.

68 **Meanwhile, in New York State:** Spectrum News, "The New
York Prison-to-Shelter Pipeline," NY1, February 27, 2018,
https://www.ny1.com/nyc/all-boroughs/politics/2018/02/27
/ny1-investigation-more-inmates-released-upstate-prisons-go
ing-into-nyc-shelter-system.

68 **Nationwide, men:** Paola Scommegna, "U.S. Has World's Highest Incarceration Rate," Population Reference Bureau (website),
report, August 10, 2012, https://www.prb.org/resources/u-s
-has-worlds-highest-incarceration-rate/.

68 **That is, it was nearly:** The Sentencing Project (website), "Fact Sheet: Incarcerated Women and Girls," report, May 12, 2022, https://www.sentencingproject.org/publications/incarcerated-women-and-girls/.

69 **An extensive study:** S. Belenko et al., "Substance Abuse and the Prison Population: A Three-Year Study by Columbia University Reveals Widespread Substance Abuse Among Offender Population," *Corrections Today* 60, no. 6 (October 1998), in the annotation, https://www.ojp.gov/ncjrs/virtual-library/abstracts/substance-abuse-and-prison-population-three-year-study-columbia.

69 **These drugs come at a high premium:** Olivia Fields, "The Never-Ending Drug Hustle Behind Bars," The Marshall Project (website), November 7, 2019, https://www.themarshallproject.org/2019/11/07/the-never-ending-drug-hustle-behind-bars.

69 **Mental health professional Mary Buser:** Mary Buser, phone interview with author, July 23, 2020.

69 **A California-based study:** Nancy Nicosia, John M. MacDonald, and Jeremy Arks, "Disparities in Criminal Court Referrals to Drug Treatment and Prison for Minority Men," *American Journal of Public Health* 103, no. 6 (June 2013): e77–e84, https://www.ncbi.nlm.nih.gov/pmc/articles/PMC3670657/ .

70 **In the nation's prisons:** Wanda Bertrum and Wendy Sawyer, "Prisons and Jails Will Separate Millions of Mothers from Their Children in 2021," Prison Policy Initiative (website), blog, May 5, 2021, https://www.prisonpolicy.org/blog/2021/05/05/mothers-day-2021/.

70 **In 2017, two-thirds reported:** Suzanne Singer, "The Women's Jail at Rikers Island Is Named for My Grandmother. She Would Not Be Proud," *New York Times*, May 12, 2020, https://www.nytimes.com/2020/05/12/opinion/womens-jail-rikers-island-covid.html.

70 **Most facilities lack the resources:** Sawyer and Wagner, "Mass Incarceration."

70 **Some jails have also been denying:** ACLU, *Over-Jailed and Un-Treated: How the Failure to Provide Treatment for Substance Use in Prisons and Jails Fuels the Overdose Epidemic*, 2021, accessed on May 20, 2023, https://www.aclu.org/wp-content /uploads/legal-documents/20210625-mat-prison_1.pdf.

71 **There was reportedly a serial rapist:** James C. McKinley Jr., "In Rape Case at Rikers: Did Guards Turn a Blind Eye?," *New York Times*, September 21, 2017, https://www.nytimes .com/2017/09/21/nyregion/rikers-rape-case-guards.html.

71 **When it opened in 1988:** New York City Department of Correction, "Rose M. Singer Center," *Corrections Newsletter*, July 1988, http://www.correctionhistory.org/html/searches/cnws rosie.html.

71 **Since then, however:** Singer, "The Women's Jail."

74 **"America's open frontier":** Adam Liptak, "Illegal Globally, Bail for Profit Remains in U.S.," *New York Times*, January 29, 2008, https://www.nytimes.com/2008/01/29/us/29bail.html.

75 **On April 1, 2019:** Ames Grawert and Noah Kim, "The Facts on Bail Reform and Crime Rates in New York State," Brennan Center for Justice (website), report, March 22, 2022, https:// www.brennancenter.org/our-work/research-reports/facts-bail -reform-and-crime-rates-new-york-state.

76 **When New York scaled back:** Tysheim Jenkins, "Commentary: Rolling Back Bail Reform Will Perpetuate Systemic Racism," *Times Union*, June 8, 2020, http://www.timesunion .com/opinion/article/Commentary-Rolling-back-bail-reform -will-15325439.php.

FIVE: Law Enforcement

79 **Though the Department of Justice defines law:** Bureau of Justice Statistics (website), "Law Enforcement," https://bjs.ojp .gov/topics/law-enforcement.

79 **New York Police Department's police commissioner:** Dean Meminger, "Commissioner Dermot Shea Apologizes for Systemic Racism in the NYPD," NY1, February 24, 2021, Spectrum News, https://www.ny1.com/nyc/manhattan/pub lic-safety/2021/02/24/commissioner-shea-apologizes-for-sys temic-racism-in-the-nypd.

80 **"Southern cities like New Orleans":** Alex S. Vitale, *The End of Policing* (New York: Verso, 2017).

80 **When slavery was abolished:** History Channel (website), "Black Codes," editorial, January 19, 2023, https://www.history .com/topics/black-history/black-codes.

80 **"They relentlessly and systematically":** NAACP (website), "The Origins of Modern Day Policing," https://naacp.org /find-resources/history-explained/origins-modern-day-policing.

80 **Boston Mayor Samuel Eliot:** Vitale, *End of Policing*, p. 70.

81 **"The late 19th century was":** Olivia Waxman, "How the U.S. Got Its Police Force," *Time*, May 18, 2017, https://time .com/4779112/police-history-origins/.

81 **largest municipal police force:** NYPD (website), "About NYPD," https://www.nyc.gov/site/nypd/about/about-nypd /about-nypd-landing.page.

82 **At the same time, fires erupted across:** Diogomaye Ndiaye, "How the Bronx Burnt," Bronx River Alliance (website), report, September 14, 2020, https://bronxriver.org/post/greenway /how-the-bronx-burned.

82 **By the end of the decade:** Vera Institute of Justice (web-site), ERA report on community policing in 72nd precinct,

November 1984, https://www.vera.org/publications/the-com
munity-patrol-officer-program-a-pilot-program-in-communi
ty-oriented-policing-in-the-72nd-precinct-progress-report.

82 **By the 1980s:** Alan M. Webber, "Crime and Management: An
Interview with New York City Police Commissioner Lee P.
Brown," *Harvard Business Review*, May-June 1991, https://hbr
.org/1991/05/crime-and-management-an-interview-with
-new-york-city-police-commissioner-lee-p-brown.

82 **"Policing changed from a preventative":** William Bratton,
"Community Policing and Change," Project for Public Spaces
(website), https://www.pps.org/article/bratton.

83 **In the summer of 1984:** Vera Institute of Justice (website),
"The Community Patrol Officer Program."

84 **"The precinct commanders":** Pat Russo, interview with author, March 11, 2022, Flatbush, Brooklyn.

84 **A hot spot:** U.S. Department of Housing and Urban Development (HUD), Office of Policy Development and Research,
"Neighborhoods and Violent Crime," HUD User (website), report, Summer 2016, https://www.huduser.gov/portal/periodi
cals/em/summer16/highlight2.html.

85 **This phenomenon, termed:** Columbia University, Center for
Spatial Research, "Project: Million Dollar Blocks," https://c4sr
.columbia.edu/projects/million-dollar-blocks.

85 **By 1989, the community:** J. E. McElroy, C. A. Cosgrove, and
S. A. Sadd, "CPOP: The Research: An Evaluative Study of
the New York City Community Patrol Officer Program," Office of Justice Programs (website), report, 1990, https://www
.ojp.gov/ncjrs/virtual-library/abstracts/cpop-research-evalua
tive-study-new-york-city-community-patrol.

85 **By 1991, every:** Webber, "Crime and Management."

86 **three main barriers:** Noah Brook, "What's the Deal with Community Policing?," Public Works Partners (website), report,

August 18, 2022, https://web.archive.org/web/2023012906 5228/https://www.publicworkspartners.com/2022/08/18 /whats-the-deal-with-community-policing/.

86 **First described in:** George L. Kelling and James Q. Wilson, "Broken Windows," *The Atlantic*, March 1982, https://www .theatlantic.com/magazine/archive/1982/03/broken-win dows/304465/.

86 **Kelling later wrote:** George Kelling, "Don't Blame My 'Broken Windows' Theory for Poor Policing," *Politico*, August 11, 2015, https://www.politico.com/magazine/story/2015/08/bro ken-windows-theory-poor-policing-ferguson-kelling-121268/.

87 **As Bratton wrote in:** William Bratton, *The Turnaround: How America's Top Cop Reversed the Crime Epidemic* (New York: Random House, 1998), p. x.

87 **more than 80 percent:** Floyd v. City of N.Y., 959 F. Supp. 2d 540 (S.D.N.Y. 2013), 559, CaseText, https://casetext.com /case/floyd-v-city-of-ny-2.

87 **"Stop-and-frisk became":** Ames Grawert and James Cullen, "Fact Sheet: Stop and Frisk's Effect on Crime in New York City," Brennan Center for Justice (website), report, October 7, 2016, https://www.brennancenter.org/our-work/research-re ports/fact-sheet-stop-and-frisks-effect-crime-new-york-city.

87 **But there was no evidence:** Cornell Law School (website), "Stop and Frisk," report, accessed July 8, 2022, https://www .law.cornell.edu/wex/stop_and_frisk.

87 **"Given this large-scale":** James Cullen, "Ending New York's Stop-and-Frisk Did Not Increase Crime," Brennan Center for Justice (website), opinion, April 11, 2016, https://www.bren nancenter.org/our-work/analysis-opinion/ending-new-yorks -stop-and-frisk-did-not-increase-crime.

88 **In 2013, a federal judge:** Joseph Goldstein, "Judge Rejects New York's Stop-and-Frisk Policy," *New York Times*, August 12,

2013, https://www.nytimes.com/2013/08/13/nyregion/stop
-and-frisk-practice-violated-rights-judge-rules.html.

90 **Members of the legendary:** *Wu-Tang Clan: Of Mics and Men*, Showtime, 2019, https://www.sho.com/wu-tang-clan-of
-mics-and-men.

90 **By 2017, New York City:** Inimai M. Chettair and James Cullen, "NYC Can Still Boast Being Safest Big City," Brennan Center for Justice (website), editorial, December 9, 2015, https://
www.brennancenter.org/our-work/analysis-opinion/nyc-can
-still-boast-being-safest-big-city.

91 **Gang wars among:** Kyle Lawson, " 'Everyone Knew This Was Going to Happen'—More Blood Shed in Park Hill; Neighbors Fed Up with Nighttime Activities," *Silive* (news app), March 16, 2021, https://www.silive.com/crime/2020/11/everyone-knew
-this-was-going-to-happen-more-bloodshed-in-park-hill-neigh
bors-fed-up-with-nighttime-activities.html.

91 **In November 2020:** Kerry Burke and John Annese, "Woman, 52, shot in head in lobby of Staten Island apartment building," *New York Daily News*, November 11, 2020, https://
www.nydailynews.com/new-york/nyc-crime/ny-woman-shot
-head-20201117-wvt3oyrhnzcntlex5tmqzb5jkq-story.html.

91 **A young Golden Gloves:** Joseph Ostapiuk, "What We Know: Two Clifton Shootings Leave One Dead, Another Injured," *Staten Island Live*, July 27, 2020, https://www.silive.com/news/2020
/07/what-we-know-two-clifton-shootings-leave-1-dead-another
-injured.html.

91 **Many housing developments:** Edward Conlon, *Blue Blood* (New York: Riverhead Books, 2005), p. 4.

93 **"We prepare police officers":** Roge Karma, "We Train Police to Be Officers," *Vox* (news app), July 31, 2020, https://www
.vox.com/2020/7/31/21334190/what-police-do-defund-abolish
-police-reform-training.

95 **"It turns your stomach"**: Gary Stark, interview with author, Park Hill Cops & Kids gym, April 29, 2021, Park Hill, Staten Island.

97 **A 2017 study conducted:** Rich Morin et al., *Behind the Badge*, "3. Police and the Community," Pew Research Center (website), report, January 11, 2017, https://www.pewresearch.org /social-trends/2017/01/11/police-and-the-community/.

97 **The sixth cause:** NAACP (website), "Criminal Justice Fact Sheet," accessed on February 3, 2023, https://naacp.org/re sources/criminal-justice-fact-sheet.

SIX: An "Award-Winning" Jail

101 **Costing $42 million:** David Showers, "Garland Country OKs Final Budget," *Sentinel-Record*, December 21, 2015, https:// www.hotsr.com/news/2015/dec/21/garland-county-oks-fi nal-budget-2015122/.

102 **In 2021, the American:** Steven Mross, "GCDC Leads Nation with Most Certified Jail Officers," *Sentinel-Record*, January 10, 2021, https://www.hotsr.com/news/2021/jan/10/gcdc-leads-na tion-with-most-certified-jail/.

112 **An article in a magazine of the:** Lorna Collier, "Incarceration Nation," *Monitor on Psychology* 45, no. 9 (October 2014): 56, https://www.apa.org/monitor/2014/10/incarceration#:~:text =Mental%20illness%20among%20today's%20inmates,ram pant%20and%20often%20co%2Doccurring.

112 **Jails in New York City, Los Angeles:** Matt Ford, "America's Largest Mental Hospital Is a Jail," *The Atlantic*, June 8, 2015, https://www.theatlantic.com/politics/archive/2015/06/amer icas-largest-mental-hospital-is-a-jail/395012/.

113 **"Those cells were not":** Gregory Cook, phone interview with author, August 5, 2021.

114 **"A lot of people":** Gregory Cook, phone interview with author, May 2021.

114 **"There had been some"**: Gregory Cook, email interview with author, April 13, 2023.

SEVEN: The Bureaucrats

115 **With an estimated:** NYC Department of Design and Construction, "20th Anniversary," accessed February 2020, website no longer available.

116 **Participating in the interview:** Jamie Torres Springer, Thomas Foley, and Michaela Metcalfe, phone interview with author, February 11, 2020, Department of Design and Construction, Long Island City.

117 **"I think a lot of architects"**: Gregory Cook, email to author, February 24, 2023.

118 **He also pointed out that:** Ian Michaels, email to author, July 22, 2021.

119 **Today it houses:** New York City (website), "The David N. Dinkins Manhattan Building," Department of Citywide Administrative Services, fact sheet, accessed October 3, 2022, https://www.nyc.gov/site/dcas/business/dcasmanagedbuild ings/david-n-dinkins-manhattan-municipal-building.page.

120 **Glazer greeted me with a kind:** Elizabeth Glazer, interview with author, February 7, 2020, Mayor's Office of Criminal Justice, 1 Centre Street, New York City.

EIGHT: The Neighbors

125 **Sixteen men died:** Michael Wilson and Chelsia Rose Marcius, "16 Men Died in N.Y.C. Jails Last Year. Who Were They?," *New York Times*, January 31, 2022, https://www.nytimes .com/2022/01/28/nyregion/rikers-island-prisoner-deaths.html.

127 **"I do not support"**: Asian American Federation, "AAF 2021 Mayoral Forum," April 27, 2021, YouTube video, 1:38:41, https://www.youtube.com/watch?v=794jxBj__OA&t=1514s.

127 **In January 2022, hundreds:** Kimberly Gonzalez, Sara Dorn, and Sahalie Donaldson, "A Timeline on the Closure of Rikers Island," City and State of New York (website), December 14, 2022, https://www.cityandstateny.com/politics/2022/12/time line-closure-rikers-island/376662/.

127 **With a tough-on-crime:** City of New York (website), "Closing Rikers Island," news update, January 5, 2023, https://rikers .cityofnewyork.us/.

127 **It seemed unlikely to skeptics:** Rachel Vick, "DOC Casts doubt on city closing Rikers by 2027," *Queens Daily Eagle*, January 3, 2023, https://council.nyc.gov/carlina-rivera/2023/01 /03/queens-daily-eagle-doc-casts-doubt-on-city-closing-rik ers-by-2027/.

130 **While Manhattan's Chinatown:** Census Reporter (website), "NYC-Manhattan Community District 3—Chinatown & Lower East Side PUMA NY," report, 2021, https://censusre porter.org/profiles/79500US3603809-nyc-manhattan-com munity-district-3-chinatown-lower-east-side-puma-ny/.

131 **During Mayor Ed Koch's:** Maurice Carroll, "Jail Near Chinatown Is Approved by 7 to 4 by Board of Estimate," *New York Times*, December 3, 1982, https://www.nytimes .com/1982/12/03/nyregion/jail-near-chinatown-is-approved -by-7-to-4-by-board-of-estimate.html.

132 **"People said we're just":** Jan Lee, phone interview with author, November 3, 2020.

132 **"People don't want any kind":** George Carlin, *Jammin' in New York*, 1992, originally aired on HBO, https://www.you tube.com/watch?v=9NrnJGFlJBE.

133 **"Because individuals":** Kate Walz, "The Color of Power: How Local Control Over Affordable Housing Shapes America," Shriver Center on Poverty Law (website), September 14, 2018, https://www.povertylaw.org/article/the-color-of-power

-how-local-control-over-affordable-housing-shapes-amer
ica-2/.

133 **During the last 20 years:** Jacqueline Rabe Thomas, "Separated by Design: How Some of America's Richest Towns Fight Affordable Housing," *ProPublica*, May 22, 2019, https://www .propublica.org/article/how-some-of-americas-richest-towns -fight-affordable-housing.

133 **"People would accuse us":** Lee, interview.

134 **"The idea was to enlist":** Anthony Flint, *Wrestling with Moses: How Jane Jacobs Took on New York's Master Builder and Transformed the American City* (New York: Random House, 2009), p. 52.

134 **They then built Stuyvesant Town:** Flint, *Wrestling with Moses*, pp. 52–53.

134 **Under the federal Housing Act:** Flint, *Wrestling with Moses*, p. 55.

135 **"Minority, low-income, and indigenous":** U.S. Environmental Protection Agency (website), "Power Plants and Neighboring Communities," report, February 16, 2023, https://www .epa.gov/airmarkets/power-plants-and-neighboring-commu nities.

135 **In majority-Black communities:** Lylla Younes, Ava Kofman, Al Shaw, and Lisa Song, "Poison in the Air," *ProPublica*, November 2, 2021, https://www.propublica.org/article/toxmap-poison -in-the-air.

136 **increases in asthma morbidity:** B. Ostro et al., "Air Pollution and Exacerbation of Asthma in African-American Children in Los Angeles," *Epidemiology* 12, no. 2 (2000): 200–208, https:// pubmed.ncbi.nlm.nih.gov/11246581/.

136 **"Your future is in this":** Lee, interview.

136 **When Oakes handed over her:** Iakowi:he'ne' (Melissa) Oakes, interview with author, March 23, 2021, New York City.

138 **In March 2021:** *Neighbors United Below Canal et al., Petitioners-Respondents, v. Mayor Bill de Blasio et al.*, Index No. 100250/20 (N.Y. App. Div. 2021), https://casetext.com /case/neighbors-united-below-canal-v-mayor-bill-deblasio.

NINE: The Prison Abolitionists

140 **"Being in jail is a very":** Raphael Sperry, phone interview with author, February 8, 2020.

142 **"The Prison Boycott":** Raphael Sperry, "Prison Design Boycott Campaign," Now What?! (website), November 27, 2018, https://www.nowwhat-architexx.org/articles/2018/11/27 /prison-design-boycott-campaign.

142 **"The supermax represents":** Michael Sorkin, "Drawing the Line: Architects and Prisons," *The Nation*, August 27, 2013, https://www.thenation.com/article/archive/drawing-line-ar chitects-and-prisons/.

142 **"Architecture is never nonpolitical":** Michael Sorkin, interview by Aleksandra Wagner, Lebbeus Woods (website), originally appearing in *Čovjek I Prostor* (*Man and Space*), a journal of the Croatian Architects Association, nos. 7-8 (2006): pp. 39–47, https://lebbeuswoods.wordpress.com/2007/11/26/mich ael-sorkin-interview-by-aleksandra-wagner/.

144 **In a 2019 published advisory opinion:** American Institute of Architects (website), Code of Ethics and Professional Conduct, 2019, p. 3, https://content.aia.org/sites/default/files/2020-02 /DPSR_Advisory_Opinion_200102.pdf.

144 **They booed him:** Sperry, interview.

144 **"Architects should not":** Michael Kimmelman, "There's No Reason for an Architect to Design a Death Chamber," *New York Times*, June 12, 2020, https://www.nytimes.com/2020/06/12 /arts/design/architects-prison-death-chamber.html.

144 **"[Our belief in prison abolition]"**: Ruth Wilson Gilmore and James Kilgore, "The Case for Abolition," The Marshall Project (website), June 19, 2019, https://www.themarshallproject .org/2019/06/19/the-case-for-abolition.

145 **"Abolitionists, therefore"**: John Washington, "What Is Prison Abolition?," *The Nation*, July 31, 2018, https://www.thenation .com/article/archive/what-is-prison-abolition/.

145 **Davis is a distinguished professor**: Humanities Office, University of California, Santa Cruz (website), "Angela Y. Davis," faculty information, accessed May 7, 2023, https://human ities.ucsc.edu/academics/faculty/index.php?uid=aydavis.

146 **In 1997, Davis**: Critical Resistance (website), accessed December 9, 2022, https://criticalresistance.org/mission-vision /history/.

146 **Her seminal book**: Angela Y. Davis, *Are Prisons Obsolete?* (New York: Seven Stories Press, 2003), p. 21, https://collective liberation.org/wp-content/uploads/2013/01/Are_Prisons_Ob solete_Angela_Davis.pdf.

146 **"everlasting as the sun"**: Davis, *Are Prisons Obsolete?*, p. 24.

147 **Offenders should "fully account"**: Alex S. Vitale, quoted in Washington, "What Is Prison Abolition?"

148 **The recidivism rate**: Danielle Sered, *Until We Reckon: Violence, Mass Incarceration, and a Road to Repair* (New York: New Press, 2019), pp. 44–45.

148 **Those who complete**: Sered, *Until We Reckon*, p. 134.

148 **"People are built"**: Sered, *Until We Reckon*, p. 25.

149 **"If your job is to punish"**: Danielle Sered, phone interview with author, February 24, 2021.

149 **Longtime abolitionist and organizer**: Quoted in "We Do This 'Til We Free Us': Mariame Kaba on Abolishing Police, Prisons, & Moving Toward Justice," Democracy Now! Productions,

March 5, 2021, YouTube video, https://www.youtube.com /watch?v=_xdOirL2V0o.

150 **"Ultimately, abolition is a practical":** Gilmore and Kilgore, "The Case for Abolition."

150 **"I am not a reformist":** MiAngel Cody, phone interview with author, February 4, 2021.

151 **"I, like many":** Ruth Wilson Gilmore, interview by Chenjurai Kumanyika, *The Intercept*, June 10, 2020, https://theintercept .com/2020/06/10/ruth-wilson-gilmore-makes-the-case-for -abolition/.

151 **"Decriminalizing mental-health episodes":** Washington, "What Is Prison Abolition?"

151 **"Criminalizing addiction through drug laws":** Washington, "What Is Prison Abolition?"

152 **Sometimes force must be used:** Christians for the Abolition of Prisons (website), "FAQ," accessed June 8, 2022, https:// christiansforabolition.org/faq/.

153 **"The funds that were rapidly located":** Woods Ervin, email interview with author, November 17, 2022.

153 **"When I helped launch":** Janos Marton, phone interview with author, January 5, 2021.

154 **According to the Lippman report:** Jonathan Lippman et al., *A More Just New York City: Independent Commission on New York City Criminal Justice and Incarceration Reform*, commission report, April 2017, page 2, https://static1.squarespace .com/static/5b6de4731aef1de914f43628/t/5b96c6f81ae6cf5 e9c5f186d/1536607993842/Lippman%2BCommission %2BReport%2BFINAL%2BSingles.pdf.

154 **"I'm an abolitionist, but":** Brandon Holmes (New York campaign coordinator at JustLeadershipUSA), phone interview with author, June 12, 2020.

155 **They advocate for:** Action Network (website), Petition: Close

Rikers Without Building New Jails in NYC, online petition to be submitted to New York City Council, n.d., https://actionnetwork.org/petitions/b34f77de17a8eb0320583feea17ef27a63fb5e5d.

156 **"That comes from people":** Glenn Martin, phone interview with author, September 16, 2020.

156 **"I think it's a mistake":** Sperry, interview.

156 **The group urged architects:** American Institute of Architects, New York Chapter (website), statement, September 30, 2020, https://www.aiany.org/advocacy/aiany-criminal-justice-facilities-statement/.

156 **"We see this as a beginning":** Kim Yao, phone interview with author, October 5, 2020.

157 **"It's fantastic":** Sperry, interview.

157 **"There were varying degrees":** Frank Greene, phone interview with author, October 5, 2020.

158 **The AIA had finally changed:** American Institute of Architects (website), "AIA Board of Directors Commits to Advancing Justice Through Design," press release, December 11, 2020, https://www.aia.org/press-releases/6356669-aia-board-of-directors-commits-to-advancin.

TEN: The Future

161 **"I think that we need to":** Square One Project (website), "Elizabeth Glazer," https://squareonejustice.org/expert/elizabeth-glazer/.

162 **"imagining a future for justice":** Square One Project (website), "Who We Are," https://squareonejustice.org/about/.

162 **which promotes public safety:** Vital City (website), "About Us," https://www.vitalcitynyc.org/about.

162 **The answer is:** Pat Russo, interview with author, March 11, 2022, Flatbush, Brooklyn.

165 **This new position:** Gregory Cook, phone interview with author, November 2, 2022.

165 **Designing Justice + Designing Spaces:** Designing Justice + Designing Spaces (website), accessed February 25, 2023, https://designingjustice.org.

165 **"You can't reform a system":** Deanna Van Buren (cofounder of Designing Justice + Designing Spaces), phone interview with author, June 15, 2021.

166 **"The local jail is the most":** Nagel, *The New Red Barn*, p. 159.

166 **"These facilities do not reduce":** Nagel, *The New Red Barn*, p. 144.

166 **"physical plants in":** Nagel, *The New Red Barn*, p. 1.

166 **"The correctional monuments":** Nagel, *The New Red Barn*, p. 182.

167 **ballooned 700 percent:** NAACP (website), "Criminal Justice Fact Sheet," accessed February 9, 2023, https://naacp.org/resources/criminal-justice-fact-sheet.

168 **"Kudos to Molina":** Katie Honan, "Adams Gives Himself 'Solid B+' on First Year. How Has He Done?," *The City*, December 27, 2022, https://www.thecity.nyc/2022/12/27/23524414/eric-adams-administration-first-year.

168 **"You have to":** Honan, "Adams Gives Himself."

About the Author

EVA FEDDERLY's investigative reporting has been published in *Architectural Digest*, *New York* magazine, the *Christian Science Monitor*, *Esquire*, and *Courthouse News*, where she reported hundreds of news-breaking stories on the American legal system. She is a graduate of the University of California, Berkeley, and Harvard University, and lives in New York City and New Orleans.